SEX AND THE TEENAGER

Kieran Sawyer, S.S.N.D.

SEX AND THE TEENAGER

choices and decisions

Ave Maria Press AVE Notre Dame, Indiana

Nihil Obstat:
Robert Gotcher, Ph.D.
Associate Professor, Sacred Heart School of Theology
Censor

Imprimatur:
The Most Reverend Timothy M. Dolan, S.T.D., D.D.
Archbishop of Milwaukee

Given at Milwaukee, WI on 17 July 2007.

The Nihil Obstat and Imprimatur are official declarations that a book or pamphlet is free of doctrinal or moral error. No implication is contained therein that those who have granted the Nihil Obstat and Imprimatur agree with its contents, opinions, or statements expressed.

Founded in 1865, Ave Maria Press is a ministry of the United States Province of Holy Cross.

www.avemariapress.com

ISBN-10 1-64680-200-4   ISBN-13 978-1-64680-200-5

Cover and text design by Brian C. Conley.

Printed and bound in the United States of America.

This book is my gift of love
to all teens and soon-to-be teens
and to the parents, teachers, and youth ministers
whose role it is
to guide them toward
positive, life-giving choices and decisions.

CONTENTS

1

TODAY'S TEENS AND THEIR CHOICES

Choices! Choices! Choices! You face a plethora of choices every single day.

This book is about the choices you are making and will make in the area of sexuality. These important choices always have far-reaching emotional, spiritual, and physical consequences.

As the Catechism of the Catholic Church reminds us, "Sexuality affects all aspects of the human person in the unity of body and soul" (2332). The vocation to chastity—the successful integration of sexuality within a person—is a common one to all people, no matter their state in life.

This book will help you to understand why chastity is a good decision for you.

The book is really more about sexual relationships than about sex. It assumes you already know the basic biological facts about male and female anatomy. It focuses on the choices and decisions you make each day that affect your relationships, especially your relationships with the opposite sex.

This book is meant to help you make choices and decisions that build beautiful, long-lasting love relationships.

Note to Parents

This chapter explains to the teens that the program presented in Sex and the Teenager is really more about relationships than about sex. It assumes that teens already know the basic biological facts about sex, and focuses on the choices they make each day that affect their relationships, especially their relationships with the opposite sex. It presents a number of letters written by actual teens which show that there is no such thing as a "typical teen," and that young people vary widely in their moral standards and in their experiences of dating and male-female relationships. The chapter points out that choices and decisions in the area of sexuality have far-reaching emotional, spiritual, and physical consequences. It offers all teens help in making life-giving, positive choices.

Moral Systems—A Survey

As you make choices in the area of sexuality, you will be influenced to a greater or lesser degree by each of three moral systems: social standards, basic moral norms, and personal moral convictions.

The phrase social standards refers to the conduct that seems to be acceptable to most of the people in the broader society around us. This is the morality of "everybody says," "everybody thinks," and "everybody is doing it." We find it portrayed in movies, television programs, songs, news broadcasts, jokes, locker talk, and so on. According to this moral system, sexual activity is acceptable in any relationship as long as both parties are willing or "consenting" and no one seems to be getting hurt. The standards are somewhat stricter for females than for males: For example it is less acceptable for a woman to have many sexual partners than for a man.

The phrase basic moral norms refers to the sexual morality you were taught by your parents and religious leaders. These norms, which are based on natural law, on the Sacred Scriptures, and on the teachings of the Church, tell us that sexual intercourse, as well as the sexual activity that leads to intercourse, is acceptable only within a committed marriage relationship. Basic morality requires that we respect our own sexuality and that of others, and that we show this respect in the way we act, the clothes we wear, the jokes we tell, the songs we listen to, the shows we watch, the things we read, and the language we use. It requires that we avoid any circumstances—persons, places, or activities—that would cause us to deviate from the norms. It also requires that we accept responsibility for the consequences of whatever choices we make.

The phrase personal moral convictions refers to the sexual moral code that each person follows in his or her day-to-day life. One of the goals of this book is to help you to deepen your convictions regarding this very personal and important aspect of your life. To do this, you will have to be aware of the subtly pervasive influence of the everybody-does-it social standards and to understand the Church's basic moral norms and the reasons behind them. Finally, you will have to do some serious reflecting on your own moral ideals and on how faithful you are in living up to them. It is hoped that this program will help you to develop personal moral convictions that are based on scripture and Catholic Christian moral teachings. Our prayer is that each young person who reads this book will firmly choose to save sex for marriage.

Choices, Freedom, and Consequences

To understand this program, it is important that you understand three central concepts: choices, freedom, and consequences.

Choices

Life is full of choices.

What classes should you take? What college should you apply to? Should you get a part-time job? What should you wear today? Should you go to the dance with a date or with your friends? Do you want to play on the basketball team this year? What time should you leave the party?

Some choices are yours to make. Some choices are made for you by others. Sometimes it's easy to decide which choice is best for you. Sometimes it seems impossible to choose. Some decisions have long-range consequences that affect your whole life. Others don't really matter one way or another. Some choices are made spontaneously. Some take days and weeks of thought and prayer and are made only after seeking out the advice of another. Some choices are moral and good. Some choices are immoral and sinful.

The focus of this book is in an area of choice that almost always has life-changing consequences—sex and sexual relationships.

Freedom

Are you free to make your own choices about sexual relationships? The answer is both yes and no.

Yes, you are free to decide for yourself the important sexual questions—who to date, how far to go, whether to have sex, when to break up, what to do if a pregnancy occurs, when and who to marry. Even if they wanted to, your parents, teachers, and religious leaders have little power to make these decisions for you.

And no. You are not free, not totally. Your freedom is restricted in many ways. You are not free to violate another person's freedom. You are not free to disregard the natural law, the laws of God, or the laws of the state. You are not free to avoid the consequences of your choices.

Choosing freely doesn't mean doing whatever you feel like doing. Freedom is one of God's greatest gifts, but it is a gift that must be used with respect and care. God invites us to play a part in building our own lives and the lives of others. God trusts us with the gift of freedom, even though he knows that we might sometimes misuse it.

To make a really free choice takes some careful (and prayerful!) thinking. You have to include in your decision-making everyone who is affected by your choice. For decisions about sex, those affected by your choice include the person you have sex with, your parents and the parents of your sexual partner, your peers, God, a baby who might be conceived, and many others.

Consequences

Freedom always implies responsibility. Whenever we make free choices, we are responsible for the now and foreseeable consequences of our choices. Because sexual activity has such important consequences for so many people there are commandments and laws and parental rules governing it. You will find it easier to accept the rules if you realize that their purpose is to protect your freedom, not restrict it. These rules are also in place to protect the freedom of others.

> The virtue of chastity blossoms in friendship. . . . Whether it develops between persons of the same or opposite sex, friendship represents a great good for all.
>
> —*CCC*, 2347

The rules say, for instance, that no one is free to force sex on someone else, that adults are not free to use children for sex, that neither parent is free to abandon a child they have conceived, that a married person is not free to have sex with someone other than his or her spouse. It's quite easy to see that rules like these are meant to protect someone's freedom. But it may be harder for you to understand that parental restrictions—what age you can date, who you can go out with, where you can go, when you have to be home—are also meant to protect your freedom of choice.

Yes, you are free to make your own choices about sexual relationships. Those who love you—especially God—hope that you will make responsible, life-giving choices. The good choices you make today can be steppingstones to a rich life of love, happiness, and peace. The wrong choices can destroy your freedom and trap you in circumstances and situations in which you would be far from free.

Letters from Teens

The following letters all came from teens who were asked to write anonymous letters about their experiences with dating, relationships, and sex. The teens wrote about everything from going on a first date to going all the way, from never being asked out, to always being dumped. Each letter is unique; yet every letter reveals a person who wants to love and be loved. The teens realize at a very deep level that love is the only thing that will make their lives worth living. They also want to avoid being hurt by love or using love as an excuse to hurt someone else.

One of the things that makes the search for love so difficult is that society—especially the media—seems to tell young people that the only route to love and happiness is through sex. Many feel pressured into living up to the sexual expectations of society. The letters the young people have written show that premature sexual experiences has not been a source of real happiness for them. Rather, it has often been the cause of deep emotional and spiritual pain.

Though the letters have not been edited, all the names mentioned in the letters are changed.

> We'd been friends for a couple of years before we actually started going out. He was always popular at school, and I'd liked him for so long that when we actually did start going out it was like a dream come true. I was in love for the first time in my life, and it felt great. Just hearing his voice or seeing his smile would make me forget everything else. Falling in love with him made me fall in love with life.
>
> TERESA—15

> Brian is the first guy I've really loved. We went to grade school together and live right across the street from each other. Ever since we were in sixth grade we

liked each other. Last September, we really started dating. Our feelings were stronger than ever, and he wanted to go all the way. I had no doubt in my mind, because I really loved him and I thought he loved me, too. I thought the night we had sex was the most special night of my whole life. But after that everything was different. I kept calling him. He never called me back. I see him all the time, because we live across the street, but it is as if I don't exist anymore.

COLLEEN—16

I liked this girl and she liked me. We went out a few times, but as soon as my friends found out who I was dating, they started teasing me. Because I wanted to belong with my friends, I stopped seeing her.

BRUCE—14

I have been going out with Teri for seven months now. She's all I ever think about, and I've devoted my life to her. We've been through so many problems and hard times together, it's amazing we're still together. I love her so much. I put her life in front of mine. Whatever happens to me doesn't matter anymore, just as long as she's happy. They say that premarital sex has all these side effects and dangers, but I don't believe it. We have sex all the time and it's been so totally fulfilling for both of us. It hasn't hurt our relationship one bit.

KEN—17

I strongly believed in waiting till I got married—until I fell in love with my boyfriend. He never pressured me, which made me feel real good. He was also a virgin, so it would be the first time for both of us. I was undecided for a long time, but then I finally decided that we were going to make love and love was the key word. I decided to make love to him because I am sure I am going to spend the rest of my life with him.

WANDA—16

Right now I'm involved with this girl. We've been going out for about a year. I like her but I feel as though I've got an anchor tied to my ankle and it won't let go. I know I'm too young to get this involved with anyone. I would rather go out with different types of girls and with my friends. The problem is that I don't know how to tell her because I don't want to hurt her feelings.

RALPH—17

I've never asked a girl out for fear of being rejected. There have been many girls that I loved (or at least I thought I did) but I could never get the nerve to ask them out on a date. I even practice what to say in front of a mirror, but when the time comes, I always shy away. I feel it's impossible. I'm just too scared that she'd say "NO" and that everyone would find out and I'd be very embarrassed.

BRAD—16

I started going out with Jean about eleven months ago. I really enjoy being with her and hope to spend much of my future with her. We get along very well, especially on sexual things. We both have decided that for the time being, we're not going to have sex, but the pressure is always there. I like Jean a lot and don't want anything to happen that will hurt her or spoil the relationship.

NATHAN—17

I have always had a strong belief in God ever since I was a little girl. But I feel that God has been unfair to me. Every day I wish for happiness and for someone to fall in love with me. I pray to God for help and guidance all the time, but it seems like he doesn't hear. I have guys for friends and that is all. Everyone is always telling me how pretty I am—well, if I am so pretty, why don't I ever have a date?

SHARON—16

I decided right from the beginning I would wait until we were married before we got too intimate. But one night I set that aside, and we went all the way. Now I'm six weeks pregnant, an A student, and applying to college. I don't know what to do. We talked about abortion, but there's no way I could have it without my parents finding out. My mother would kill me and my father would cry. I don't want to kill my baby, but I really can't keep it. It would ruin everything I could ever be.

BARB—18

I had an experience a month ago that still worries me very much. I have this neighbor a few years older than me that I've admired since I was a little kid. I go over there a lot just to talk and listen to his music. But this one day I felt turned on by him, like sexually. I didn't say or do anything and neither did he, but I think we both felt it. I've been afraid to go over there since then.

JAKE—15

As of now, I am still a virgin and I want to keep it that way until I get married. I do date girls pretty often, and I often get urges to go all the way with this certain person. But I always keep in my mind that I should just hold off. It really is hard though because I get pressure from my friends, and it is supposedly "cool" to have sex. I don't know if I am ruining my relationship with certain girls or what, but I guess that is how I can tell if a girl really does love me or not. I probably sound like an out of place teenager, but I just want to stay strong and stick to my principles.

RICK—17

One night during the summer, my friend Jay invited me to a party. When we got there, I had a beer and Jay introduced me to a few of his friends, one of them being Lissa. Lissa and I were talking awhile, joking, and having fun. We both seemed to like each

> other. All of a sudden a guy came out of the bedroom with a girl, and screamed "Next!" Everyone laughed. Jay looked at us and said, "Go for it." Lissa smiled and grabbed my arm. I said to myself, "What the hell." I never saw the girl after that night.
>
> LEON—17

> I am eighteen years old and am still a virgin. I am proud of this. I am also respected for this by the people I go out with. I believe that sex is something special and should be saved for the person you plan to marry. I have been in a situation where someone I cared about wanted to have sex, but we discussed it and decided against it. I don't believe in abortion, and feel that those who choose to have sex at a young age are taking too big of a risk.
>
> EILEEN—18

If you were asked to write your own letter about love, relationships, and sexuality, which letter would most closely approximate your own experience? You may be a person who is experiencing the fun and excitement of being in love—along with the temptations that go with dating. You may be a person who has already decided that you will definitely refrain from sexual intercourse until you are married. Or, like some of the letter-writers, you may have already experienced the pain and problems that come with sex outside of marriage.

An objective of this program is to help you to tell the difference between real love and its counterfeits. Whatever your present or past experience, you are free to start now to make the kinds of choices and decisions needed to build strong, loving relationships.

Personal Journal

- What did you learn about your peers from the Sexuality Survey? What did you learn about yourself?

- Do you feel more free or more restricted regarding your choices about sexual relationships? Explain.
- Write a letter to yourself about sexuality, in the style of those listed in this chapter.

2

L.I.F.E. CHOICES: LOVE, INFATUATION, FRIENDSHIP, EXPLOITATION

Some relationships are positive and life-giving. Some are negative and destructive. It isn't always easy to know the difference, especially when you are deeply involved with someone. Sometimes a third person—a parent or good friend—is a better judge of a relationship than you are. Sometimes it isn't until months or years later, when the relationship is over, that you know whether it was good or bad for you and the other person.

This chapter looks at four basic kinds of human relationships to help you to understand your own relationships better:

LOVE A relationship characterized by commitment, unconditional acceptance, deep respect, and trust.

INFATUATION A romantic relationship involving sexual feelings and attraction. Also known as "being in love."

FRIENDSHIP A relationship between any two or more persons who trust each other and like to be together.

EXPLOITATION A relationship based on selfishness and lack of respect for the other person.

Most relationships are a combination of two or more of these basic four. For example, a romantic infatuation might be moving toward real love, a friendship relationship might include some degree of exploitation. These relationships and their combinations will be explored in more detail in the material that follows.

Note to Parents

This chapter examines four basic kinds of human relationships: Love, Infatuation, Friendship, and Exploitation. The chapter helps the teens to recognize the difference between love and infatuation, shows that the friendship aspects of a relationship can develop into love, and points out the subtle and obvious ways that all relationships can become exploitative. Most relationships combine two or more of the basic four, with a teen romance usually being a combination of I and F: infatuation and friendship. The chapter calls this the Big IF, and explains that when friendship is the dominant aspect of a dating relationship, it has a good chance of growing toward love; if infatuation is dominant, the relationship is more likely to degenerate into exploitation. It is pertinent to note that Deus Caritas Est, the first encyclical of Pope Benedict XVI, also speaks of human relationships in these four categories. The Holy Father uses the Greek words agape, eros, and philia to name the three positive relationships and refers to the negative relationship that we are calling exploitation as a relationship that is "deceptive" and "debased" and that uses sex as a mere "commodity to be used and exploited."

L.I.F.E.

Of the four types of relationships, **FRIENDSHIP**, the "F" in L.I.F.E. is the easiest of the four to understand.

Friends are the people we talk to, go places with, compete against, get in trouble with, tell secrets to, and, above all, trust. We depend on our friends for fun, laughter, and understanding. We know that our friends respect us, and we also know that they will challenge us—tell us off when we need it.

Everyone needs friends. Some of us need many friends; some prefer to have just one or two. A person can have friends of both sexes, friends of all ages, and friends with different backgrounds, religions, values, and ideas.

Having friends, belonging to a group, and being popular are key factors in the lives of teenagers—in your life. Through friendship, teens learn how to balance the conflicting claims of independence and interdependence. Friendship teaches you how to fit in with a group of peers without sacrificing your individuality.

Friendship is comfortable and easy, enriching, and fun. It is based on mutual trust, understanding, acceptance, and enjoyment. Friendship is not exclusive or possessive; it leaves the other person free. Some friendships last a lifetime. The best of them grow into love.

The "I" in L.I.F.E. stands for romantic **INFATUATION**. This book uses the word "infatuation" more broadly than its normal use to include any relationship that involves sexual attraction or sexual feelings. The "I factor" includes a spectrum of romantic relationships that include everything from just being interested in someone, to being in touch (holding hands, writing notes, making phone calls), to being emotionally involved, to being totally infatuated, to being very much "in love," to being sexually intimate.

Romantic infatuation is exciting and all-absorbing. It seeks expression in kisses, hugs, touches, and eventually sexual intercourse. It is usually characterized by exclusiveness and jealousy. When you are "in love" you often experience extremes of happiness and dejection, joy and anxiety.

Learning to deal with the awakening of sexual feelings and interests is a major challenge of adolescence. Falling in love can be one of the most exciting human experiences, and it can also be one of the most troublesome. It can make a person ecstatically happy or totally depressed. There isn't any feeling quite as wonderful as knowing that another person is in love with you. But, on the other hand, there isn't any pain quite like being rejected by a person you are in love with.

It is difficult, and important, to recognize the difference between infatuation and love in your own life experiences. Learning to do so will be one of your greatest challenges as you grow into adulthood.

The "L" in L.I.F.E. stands for **LOVE**, the most beautiful, the most rewarding, and the most challenging of all relationships. Much of your happiness in life will depend on the depth and constancy of your love relationships. It takes a whole lifetime of practice to learn how to give love and receive it.

To clarify the distinction between love and infatuation, it is helpful to think first about love as it is found in the parent-child relationship. There we see that love is characterized by wonderful qualities like commitment and understanding, acceptance and respect, sensitivity and consideration. Love is seldom easy. It usually requires a lot of patience and forgiveness and a willingness to make sacrifices. Because it takes time to forge permanent bonds of trust and understanding, a long-lasting love relationship comes only with commitment.

Love is best when it is mutual, when both persons give and both receive. But unlike friendship, a love relationship can exist even when it is mostly one-sided. You can love someone who never returns your love, or even someone who rejects it. Parental love is like that sometimes. No matter how indifferent or rebellious or selfish their children can be, parents continue to love them.

Love is the core teaching of most of the world religions. Christians believe that God is love (1 John 4:8). Jesus teaches that God's love is present in our love for one another, and that we are most like God when we love as God loves. According to the Catechism of the Catholic Church: "God himself is an eternal exchange of love, Father, Son, and Holy Spirit, and he has destined us to share in that exchange" (221).

One of the primary goals of this book is to help you to learn how the wonderful experience of a romantic relationship can lead to a true love relationship, and how to avoid the pitfalls of having infatuation degenerate into exploitation.

The "E" in the L.I.F.E. acronym, which stands for **EXPLOITATION**, refers to any relationship in which one person uses another for his or her own selfish purposes. Exploitation takes what it can get without showing any real concern or respect for the other person in the relationship.

No one likes to be used. And none of us likes to admit that we are using someone else. But we are all guilty of using others sometimes, often the people we love the most. We take our friends for granted, we abuse our parents' trust, we butter up our teachers, we blackmail our brothers and sisters, we have fun at the expense of an unpopular person, we make prank phone calls or send phony e-mails, we take advantage of somebody's weaknesses, and we manipulate people to get our own way. Serious forms of exploitation include things like theft, blackmail, and extortion.

In the realm of sexuality there are criminal forms of exploitation, and there are more common, everyday forms. Criminal exploitation includes rape, incest, pornography, prostitution, and child abuse. It is a very real possibility that someone who reads this material may have suffered from sexual abuse and knows by experience the long-range negative effects of such experiences.

But there are also other lesser forms of sexual exploitation, which many of you may have experienced either as the one exploiting or the one exploited. Examples of exploitation in the area of sexual relationships include using one boy to get back at another, taking out a popular girl to make yourself look good, ruining someone's reputation by bragging about how far you went

> The chaste person maintains the integrity of the powers of life and love placed in him [or her]. This integrity ensures the unity of the person; it is opposed to any behavior that would impair it. It tolerates neither a double life nor duplicity in speech.
>
> —*CCC*, 2338

with her or him, having sex with someone just for the experience, encouraging your date to drink so it will be easier to make advances, and going steady just so you'll always have a convenient date handy.

The Big IF—More on Basic Relationships

Most teen romances are partly infatuation and partly friendship. We can call this combination the BIG IF. How healthy and strong the relationship is usually depends on whether the "I" or "F" predominates in the relationship.

If the couple concentrates on deepening the friendship aspects of their relationship—learning to communicate, to share, to compromise, to trust one another's friends and families—then the relationship has a good chance of moving toward love. The strong sexual feelings involved in the relationships can help the individuals move beyond the natural self-centeredness of childhood toward mature caring and commitment.

On the other hand, if the primary focus of the relationship is on sexual feelings and their physical expression, the couple can very easily begin to use one another just to get emotional and sexual satisfaction. When that happens, the relationship will almost certainly degenerate into exploitation.

The best romance relationships for teens—and the safest—are those in which friendship predominates over infatuation. If the young people are friends as well as sweethearts, the respect and mutual trust that are basic to friendship help to control the sexual element in their relationship. Because they are friends, they have many common interests and many common friends. They will find many fun and interesting things to do together that will keep their relationship developing in a healthy way.

On the other hand, teenage romances that are predominately infatuation tend to be far more dangerous. Often the two people involved in such a relationship hardly know each other as friends. They may have few common interests outside each other and their feelings for each other. They spend most of their time together talking about their "love" for one another or making out. The sexual aspect of the relationship gets more and more involved, often leading prematurely to sexual intercourse.

When you are in the thick of a BIG IF relationship, it's hard to know whether you are growing toward love or slipping into exploitation. Because being in love is such a special and wonderful experience, it is easy to be fooled into thinking infatuation or even exploitation is really love. However, there is one true test: involvement in sexual activity, even short of intercourse, is a sure sign that the relationship is not healthy. Sex before marriage will most likely damage and even destroy the relationship and will certainly be harmful to both parties involved in it.

Choose Life

Love Yahweh your God
Cling to him
And obey his voice
For he has blessed you
And made you his own
Let not your heart stray
Refuse not to listen
Be not drawn away
See, before you is set
Blessings and life
Disaster and death
Choose

The decision is yours
Choose Life
So that you
And your children
May live
Live in the love
Of Yahweh your God

—Paraphrase of Deuteronomy 30

Personal Journal

- Think about a friend you have had for a long time? How has this friendship been enriching and life-giving for you?
- What are some warning signs that a relationship may be or is exploitive? How have these signs been manifested in a relationship that you have been involved in or know about?
- Name three positive steps you can take to cultivate a friendship with a person of the opposite sex.
- In what ways do you regularly "choose life"—for your family, for your friends, for the world, for future generations, for yourself?

3

DATING CHOICES

Dating in any of its many different forms (some described in this chapter) is an important learning experience. How to talk to a girl or guy, how to be yourself, how to be really interested in the other person, how to control your own sexual urges—all of these things have to be learned by experience. Dating also helps you learn about how to learn the language of touch—hand-holding, hugs, and kisses—in a way that is caring and respectful. The better and more wholesome the relationship, the more likely that you and your dating partner will agree that sexual intercourse, and the kind of sexual activity that leads to intercourse, is only appropriate within the full commitment of marriage.

Note to Parents

This chapter helps the teens to analyze the many choices involved in teenage dating and the important role dating plays in their relational development. It looks at various levels of dating and at the benefits of dating for a teen. Special emphasis is given on the positive and negative aspects of teenager parties and the responsibility teens themselves have to assure that their parties and dating experiences are in keeping with Christian moral standards.

The Dating Game

There are several variations of dating game shows on television. In the television versions there are lots of laughs, and for the most part, all parties concerned are in complete control.

In the life of a teenager, the dating game is different. Especially for younger teens, dating often includes awkward conversations and uncomfortable silences. Dating can also mark an important milepost in the relationship between teens and parents. In some ways, dating is a status symbol, with those who do date considered by their peers as being more popular than those who don't. When the dating experience is handled well, it can be a wonderful and exciting part of being a teenager. When it is played without regard for the norms of Christian morality, it can be a leading cause of teenage problems.

We are using the term "dating" to mean a special time set aside to develop (or to explore the possibility of) a romantic relationship. Three dating situations that are common among teenagers are described below:

> **Group Dating** Today's young people would probably call this kind of activity a boy-girl party or "hanging out" rather than dating. In this early form of dating, a group of guys and girls get together to share a meal, go to a movie, or do an activity together like ice skating or bowling. Sometimes the group is just friends with no exclusive ties, sometimes it is made up of several couples who are all friends with one another, sometimes there might be a combination of "singles" and "couples."
>
> There are several advantages to group dating. For those who are shy or uncomfortable in a dating situation, a group date allows a good opportunity to practice interpersonal communication skills. There is less pressure involved as a person relies on the group for support. The group date setting allows a person the chance to see what kinds of people he or she gets along with and to learn to respond to various personalities. The gathering is often chaperoned, which helps to assure that the young people are less likely to get involved in negative behaviors like drinking and drugs. Group dating is usually the preferred form of dating by parents, especially for younger teens.
>
> **Individual Dating** One to one, or individual dating, is a natural progression from group dating. The age at which teens begin individual dating varies from culture to culture, from family to family, and must always be determined in consultation with the parents of both teens involved.
>
> The decision to invite someone on a date, or to accept an invitation, is both exciting and unsettling.

Usually the dating couple are already friends who are comfortable enough with each other to be alone together. They already know one another and want to get to know each other better.

Individual dates can be fun, and they are a definite opportunity to express one's relational maturity. At this stage of dating, there should be no commitments or promises and both parties should be free to date others. This can be a problem, however, because one person often wants to move into an exclusive relationship before the other. One person can also feel he or she is "entitled" to kisses or other forms of sexual expressions that are beyond the true depths of the relationship.

Exclusive Dating In other eras, this form of dating was called "courting" or "going steady." Today it means that the couple have decided to date each other exclusively, and to spend more and more time together. They have learned to trust one another on many levels, to talk about things that are important to both of them, and to face honestly the problems and difficulties that are part of every relationship. They are comfortable being together both alone and in company.

At this stage of the relationship, the two people make a verbal commitment to one another that they will not date anyone else, at least for a time. They exchange gifts on special occasions like birthdays and Valentine's Day, often a special symbolic gift that they proudly wear as a sign that they are "going together."

Exclusive dating has wonderful benefits, but it also has many very obvious dangers. For many young people, this level of dating becomes a test of the personal moral convictions they have been developing throughout their teen years. Both parties must be willing to discuss their moral expectations honestly and openly. They must agree together to a set of safeguards that will help them to live up to their personal ideals and to withstand the internal and external pressures to become sexually active. In all of this, they will need to seek guidance and support from their parents or other trusted adults, from responsible peers, and most of all from God.

Dating in any of these forms is an important aspect of the total reality of teenage life. It provides indispensable learning experiences in all of the following areas:

- **Affection and Emotional Intimacy** A date offers a young couple an opportunity to share their feelings of warmth and affection for one another in ways that are appropriate to the relationship. Their time alone gives them a chance to enjoy one another's company, to have fun together, to talk intimately about their hopes and fears, and to share their ideas and ideals with someone who cares and listens.
- **Identity and Self-confidence** The dating experience helps teens to discover whole new aspects of their personality. Being cared for and appreciated by someone of the other gender helps teens realize the special qualities of their own masculinity or femininity. Just being asked out, or having someone accept your invitation, is a confidence builder for most teens. Being able to claim a special someone as your boyfriend or girlfriend gives a great boost in self-esteem.
- **Personal and Relational Growth** Dating is an important interpersonal learning experience. How to talk to a girl or guy, how to be yourself, how to be really interested in the other person, how to control your sexual urges—all of these things have to be learned by experience. Dating also helps you to learn how to use the language of love—hand-holding, hugs, kisses—in a way that is tender, caring, and respectful. Such personal growth is greatly impeded by the use of alcohol or other substances, which some teens use to overcome their fears and inhibitions about dating.

Dating in any of the forms described above implies that the two persons feel some degree of sexual attraction for each other. But it is false to assume that dating always, sooner or later, leads to sex. Believing that it does (or should) puts teens under a great deal of unnecessary pressure. Dating provides the opportunity for you to develop a total relationship with a person of the opposite sex, a relationship that will help you to deal with your sexual feelings and urges in a proper context. The more wholesome and better your relationship, the more likely that you and your partner will agree to delay sexual intercourse, and all of the sexual activity that leads to sexual intercourse, until you have made the full commitment of marriage.

Who Choices

What do you look for in a dating partner? How do you decide who you will go out with, either in a group or individual dating situation? What characteristics do you look for in a person as you begin or deepen a relationship with someone?

If you are like most young people, physical appearance is somewhere near the top of your list of dating criteria. Looks, build, weight, clothes, style—these are things you notice first. But they aren't nearly as important to you as friendliness, personality, and sense of humor. Teens like most to date someone who is fun to be with and easy to talk to.

Honesty and truthfulness are also high on the list of priorities for most teens. You need to know that you can trust a person you date, especially if the person becomes your boyfriend or girlfriend. You want to be sure your dating partner won't betray the secrets you share and won't talk behind your back.

Most teens care about the morals and values of the person they date. Teens with high morals concerning sex, drugs, alcohol, faith, and religion usually prefer to date a person with similar values.

Many teens are influenced by their peers in choosing a date, sometimes more than they realize. They want a boyfriend or girlfriend who has the approval of their friends, someone who fits the standards of their group. Younger teens especially find it hard to go out with someone their same-sex friends might disapprove of.

Typically, a girl likes a guy who is attentive and affectionate, but who doesn't pressure her into sex. A guy likes a girl who does not "come on" to him, and rarely respects one who does. A girl doesn't like it when a guy treats her one way when she's alone with him and is different when his friends are around. A guy feels uncomfortable when the girl he is with whispers to her friends in his presence.

Both boys and girls want to date someone who is sensitive and cares about their feelings. Most say they are looking more for a heart-to-heart caring relationship than for a relationship that includes sexual involvement.

Party, Party, Party

"I met this guy at a party."

"This really cool girl was at the party last night."

Where else? That's what parties are for—to have fun and meet people. If you're a normal teenager, you love to go to parties. But if you are a thinking teenager, you also realize that teen parties are not always wholesome, good experiences.

Most teen parties have both positive and negative aspects.

Parties are fun. They give you something to do, someplace to go. You get a bunch of friends together. Play some music. Play some games. Talk. Laugh. Act crazy. Have fun. A party is a great way to forget about school and work for a while.

Parties are the time for friends. New friends. Old friends. Girls. Guys. You go to a party because everyone else is going. You go to look and be looked at. If you're lucky, you might meet the perfect girl or guy!

But parties also have negative aspects. Some teens rely on drinking or other drugs to make the party fun. They feel they need help to relax, to get rid of their pressures, to take away their inhibitions. Everyone knows at least one teen who has been killed going to a party or coming home from one.

Parties are often a cause for disobedience and deception. Many teens have to lie to their parents in order to go to a party. Some do things at parties that are against their parents' values. Teen parties are a big problem for parents. They want you to have the party positives—fun, freedom, and friends—but they definitely want to protect you (and their property) from the party negatives.

A positive party can be a fun thing to do with a boyfriend or girlfriend. A negative party can be a disaster. The combination of an unchaperoned party, alcohol or drugs, and peer pressure has led too many teens into the dangers of casual, irresponsible, and even abusive sex.

How can you enjoy the party positives without being trapped by the party negatives? You and your friends are the only ones who can answer that question.

Personal Journal

- Dating rules regarding age, time, place, companions, frequency, and so forth vary from culture to culture, from family to family. What are the dating rules in your family? In what ways do you agree and/or disagree with them?
- Write a profile of your ideal dating partner.
- Analyze the moral standards followed by the characters in one television program you watch regularly.
- Discuss the use of alcohol and drugs in teenage dating situations. What are your personal moral convictions regarding their use?

4

THE CHOICE: TO DO OR NOT TO DO IT

If you really love someone, is it all right to say "yes" to sex? Before you answer that question, back up a step. Most teens agree that you should not have sex with someone unless you love the person. But it is harder for teens to see that if you really love someone, it is often better to say "no" to sex—or at least to say "not yet."

Love is a very elusive reality. As mentioned in Chapter 2, love can easily be confused with infatuation and even exploitation. How do you know if you really love someone? And even more puzzling, how do you know if another person really loves you? And how do you know if and when you love each other enough to express your love through sexual intercourse?

This is such an important question and has such far-reaching ramifications in your lives that both you and the person you love will want to be very sure your love is real before you engage in sexual activity.

Unfortunately, there is no simple paper and pencil test for real love. Real love can only be tested by life. When two people love each other enough to take the test life offers, they are ready to get married. Marriage isn't an absolute guarantee of love, of course, but it is a couple's best chance of knowing there is enough love—as well as enough commitment and responsibility—to sustain sexual intimacy.

A full sexual commitment is such an important decision that both civil law and Church law have a special process to publicize and formalize the commitment. That's what the marriage vow is—a formal commitment to accept all of the responsibilities that accompany a sexual union.

Among the most important responsibilities that follow from the sexual union is parenthood. In contemporary society, there is a false disconnect between sexual relationships and parenthood, which confuses the sexual thinking of today's young people. In

God's plan, sexual attraction has two primary purposes: love and procreation. According to the United States Conference of Catholic Bishops:

> The purpose of sexual desire is to draw man and woman together in the bond of marriage, a bond that is directed toward two inseparable ends: the expression of marital love and the procreation and education of children.[1]

As young people mature in their ability to relate sexually in a comfortable and responsible manner, they also ought to be gradually developing the capacity to be loving and caring parents. The decision to be sexually active should mean that you and the person you love should both be ready to assume the duties of parenthood.

So what if you really do love each other, but you haven't known each other very long, or you haven't discussed some very serious values, or you're not sure you can trust the other person completely, or you're not ready for a permanent commitment, or you aren't fully ready to be a parent? What if the relationship is developing, but still has a long way to go? What about sex then? Can't sex help to keep the relationship growing?

Contrary to what most of popular culture—especially the media—tells you, the answer is no. Statistical evidence shows that sex prior to marriage is more likely to destroy a relationship than to deepen it. Sex can trick you into thinking that intense infatuation or even exploitation is real love.

Once a couple adds sexual intimacy to their relationship, having sex can become the central focus of their lives. The other facets of their relationship often stop developing. Sooner or later one or both persons begins to feel trapped—by jealousy, or guilt, or lack of communication, or secrecy, or infidelity, or pregnancy. A relationship that may have had the potential to grow into love can be side-tracked by sex. What begins as love can end by deteriorating into exploitation.

Which brings us back to our original question: If you really love someone, is it all right to say "yes" to sex?

Unless you and the person you love are ready to take life's test of love, marriage, and parenthood, the answer is definitely NO.

When you have a special relationship with someone, and you really want that relationship to deepen and mature into love, promise yourself and each other that your relationship will not include sexual intercourse or any of the foreplay that leads to sexual intercourse until you have sealed your relationship with marriage.

The best decision is to say "no" to sex now so you can more freely, truly, and responsibly say "yes" later.

Note to Parents

Ultimately, your children must decide for themselves whether to have sex, when, and with whom. This chapter points out that making the decision to say "no" to sex before marriage is the most loving thing a person can do for himself or herself and for the one he or she loves. The reasons for this are presented in a variety of ways in this chapter. It is our hope that the message is made clear to the teens—the message that real love can only be tested by life, and that marriage, though not an absolute guarantee of love, is the best chance for a couple to know that there is enough love and commitment in their relationship to sustain sexual intimacy.

Teenage Sex: Reasons to Say "Yes" or "No"

Though the best decision is to say no to sex until marriage, the pressures you face in making a choice to have sex or not do not go away. Despite the correctness of saving sex until marriage, sooner or later you will have to decide for yourself whether you will say yes or no to premarital sex.

Obviously some teenagers are already saying yes. Many feel pressured into having sex. They think they have to do it to be popular, or to win or keep someone's love, or to prove something to someone.

Some teens have sex to make a third person jealous or to get back at their parents. Some are just curious and want to find out what it's like. Some use sex for comfort or reassurance. Many teens are drunk or high when they have sex. Some have sex just for fun. And some are cruelly forced into having sex.

Many teens say it's all right to have sex if you really love each other. But many teens have a difficult time articulating the meaning of true love and few are ready for the kind of permanent, responsible, long-term commitment that love requires.

The good news about teenagers and sex is that it is really not true that "everyone is doing it." As recent statistics point out, nearly half of junior and seniors in high school say they have never had sex. And these positive numbers are increasing, as more and more teens clearly choose to say no to sex until they are married.

Some teens choose not to have sex because they want to avoid pregnancy, AIDS, and other sexually transmitted diseases. Some feel that a heavy sexual involvement would interfere with their education or their future plans.

Some teens are afraid of being physically intimate with another person, or afraid of getting caught, or afraid of feeling guilty afterward. Some have been hurt by sex in the past and don't want to be hurt again.

Sexuality is ordered to the conjugal love of man and woman. In marriage the physical intimacy of the spouses becomes a sign and pledge of spiritual communion. Marriage bonds between baptized persons are sanctified by the sacrament.

—*CCC*, 2360

Many teens have strong religious convictions that influence how they feel about sex. They see sex as a precious gift from God and want to live their lives in accordance with God's will. Some teens choose not to have sex because they love the other person too much to risk hurting him or her. Some say no because they want to save the gift of sex for the person they will marry.

Most teens hope that they will be part of a happy, permanent marriage someday. They dream of saying a yes that will last forever to a very special someone. One of the best ways for teens to make that dream come true is to say no to sex now.

Love Waits

The following is a definition of true love by the Christian Action Council.

> Love is patient . . . Love starts with being friends—with taking time to get to know each other. It's sharing the good and bad times together.
>
> Love is kind . . . Love wants to do the best thing for another person. It's doing thoughtful things for someone else. Love never demands something that will harm you or the other person.
>
> Love will never cross the line between what's right and wrong . . . It's right to care about someone. It's wrong to put each other in danger of having to deal with hard choices . . . choices that could change both your lives, your goals and plans forever. Having sex before marriage may feel right for the moment. But the possible costs of an unexpected pregnancy, abortion, and sexually transmitted diseases—as well as the deep hurts that can come from a broken relationship—outweigh the feelings of the moment. The feelings are temporary; their consequences are long-lasting.
>
> Love waits . . . All good things are worth waiting for. Waiting to have sex until marriage is a mature decision to control your desires. Waiting allows you to build strong friendships . . . to treat yourself and others as unique and valuable individuals . . . and to treat sex as something exciting and special to be shared with one person for a lifetime. If you are getting to know someone—or are in a relationship—remember: If it's love, love waits.[2]

The Real-Love Test

The Real-Love Test is designed to help you discover if a relationship is really love or not. You will be writing your "grades" on a report card, but the Real-Love Test isn't really about written grades. It is about being honest with yourself and with someone you consider to be a boyfriend or girlfriend.

If you are "in love" right now, use the test to "grade" your current relationship. If you have a boyfriend or girlfriend, you should be able to sit down and discuss each item with him or her. If you can't talk about these things, that is probably a clear sign that you are a long way from passing the test.

If you aren't in love right now, read through the test anyway, applying it to a past relationship or some other relationship you know about. Then put the test away in a safe place so that you can find it the next time you fall in love.

Give your relationship an A, B, C, D, or F grade for each item on this test.

- **The Time Test** You've known each other for a long time, long enough to discover the many facets of the other's personality, to know the other's interests and values, to realize his or her strengths and weaknesses, to see how he or she deals with all kinds of life situations.
- **The Chemistry Test** Your whole being responds to the presence of the other. You're captivated by the way the person walks, talks, smiles, listens—even the way he or she smells. This is the easiest test to pass, and the hardest, because you can't make it happen. One day you discover it in yourself and you desperately hope that the other person feels it too.
- **The Communication Test** You can talk easily with the other person about many things. You share your thoughts and your feelings openly. You work through your disagreements and conflicts. You listen to one another and each try to understand the other's point of view.
- **The Friendship Test** You are really good friends. You like to spend time together doing many different kinds of activities. You're comfortable with each other and like being with each other's friends and families.
- **The Approval Test** The people who know you best, your parents and your friends, approve of the other person. They can see that he or she brings out the best in you. They feel that you are a better person because of this relationship.

- **The Respect Test** You are considerate and courteous in dealing with each other. You respect each other's friends, family, morals, and religious convictions. You don't use manipulation or blackmail to get your own way.
- **The Vision Test** Far from being blind, your love for the other person helps you to see very well just what kind of person he or she is. You know all about the person, good points and bad, strengths and weaknesses. You understand and accept the real person, the one behind the mask. Your relationship also helps you to see yourself in a new way.
- **The Jealousy Test** You are not possessive of the person's time or affection. You give the other person space to do things and go places without you. You encourage him or her to have other friends, both male and female.
- **The Values Test** You share common values, morals, and priorities on most of the important things in life. You discuss value questions often. You respect the other's position when it differs from yours, but you aren't afraid to challenge ideas, actions, and attitudes that you can't accept.
- **The Trust Test** You have complete confidence in the other person. You have learned from experience that you can depend on him or her to be truthful and open with you. You know that he or she will follow through on promises and commitments and support you in times of trouble.
- **The Responsibility Test** You are aware of any risks that might be involved in your relationship. You are willing and able to accept full responsibility for the consequences of your actions with one another. You will not expose your friend to unnecessary dangers of any kind.
- **The Parenthood Test** You and the other person are both open to the possibility of conceiving a child, and both of you are willing and able to assume all of the responsibilities of parenthood.
- **The Prayer Test** You pray frequently for and with each other. You see God in each other and in your

love relationship. You seem to be growing closer to God because of your love for one another. You respect one another's religious commitments and go to church together when you can.

- **The Real World Test** You are free to love one another —free from former vows and commitments, from psychological and physical impediments, from addictions. You are absolutely certain that neither of you is infected with HIV, the virus that causes AIDS, or has any other sexually transmitted disease. You are realistic about the special problems connected with any differences in age, race, family, religion, background.
- **The Tomorrow Test** You are each confident that the other will be there for you tomorrow and tomorrow and tomorrow. You are patient with each other's efforts to learn to love well. You realize that the beautiful secrets of sexual intimacy can be discovered only in a setting that provides permanence and continuity.
- **The Commitment Test** You have pledged your commitment to one another publicly in the presence of witnesses. Your relationship has been blessed by God and by your Church in a wedding. You have signed a legal contract promising to be true to one another for better or worse, for richer or poorer, in sickness and in health, until death.

Sex without love and the commitment of marriage will not make you happy. Without love and a committed marriage relationship, sex is a source of problems, worry, guilt, heartache, and disappointment. Your best assurance that your relationship is really love is marriage.

If you really love one another, say "no" to sex until you have sealed your love in marriage.

Love Is Not Blind

Love is always patient and kind
It is never jealous
Love is never boastful or conceited
It is never rude or selfish
It does not take offense

And is not resentful
Love takes no pleasure in other
people's sins
But delights in the truth
It is always ready to excuse
To trust
To hope
And to endure whatever comes
In short
There are three things that last
Faith
Hope
And Love
And the greatest of these
Is
Love

1 CORINTHIANS 13:4–7, 13 (JERUSALEM BIBLE)

Personal Journal

- What is your own definition of "real love?"
- What do you feel is the bottom-line reason for saying "no" to sex before marriage?
- What did the Real-Love Test reveal about a relationship you are currently in, were once in, or one that you know about?
- Write some of the lyrics from a favorite song or songs that express for you the meaning of real love.

5

THE UN-CHOICE: TEENAGE PREGNANCY

Pregnancy is one of God's most extraordinary miracles. When a pregnancy occurs in a loving marriage, it is one of the greatest joys and privileges a man and woman can have. As the Catechism expresses, conjugal love tends to be fruitful. "A child does not come from outside as something added on to the mutual love of the spouses, but springs from the very heart of that mutual giving, as its fruits and fulfillment" (2366).

Consider the process by which a married couple brings a new baby into the world. An act of love brings together one microscopic seed and one tiny new egg. A new life is planted in the warm, welcoming womb of the woman's body. Cells divide and multiply, becoming fingers and toes, eyes and ears, heart and lungs. In an amazing sequence of events, the tiny embryo is transformed into a human body. And nine months later a new little person is born into the world.

To choose to be a part of that miracle is one of the greatest privileges a husband and wife can have. To create a human life together is, perhaps, the most loving choice two persons can ever make. The Catechism describes this choice as one of "cooperating with the love of God the Creator" (2367).

Unfortunately, there are at least one million pregnancies that occur each year outside of a loving marriage. Most of these are teenage pregnancies. In these cases, pregnancy is usually viewed as a problem, not a miracle of love. For most pregnant teens, and for the fathers of their babies, pregnancy is experienced as a traumatic interruption in their lives. They are suddenly forced into the stark realities and hard decisions of adulthood.

This chapter focuses on the reality of pregnancy, especially teen pregnancy—the wonder, the trauma, the responsibility.

Note to Parents

Teen pregnancy, a major crisis for our society, is the subject of this chapter. Each year nearly one million American teenagers become pregnant. Every year nearly four girls in 100 between fifteen and seventeen years old have a baby. Nearly four out of ten teen pregnancies end in abortion. Of the teens who give birth, only seven in ten complete high school, and they are less likely to go on to college than other young women. The fathers of babies born to teenage mothers are usually older than the mothers.[3] Whereas pregnancies within a marriage are usually greeted with happiness and great expectations, pregnancies among unmarried teens are more likely to be viewed as a problem rather than as a miracle.

Jack and Jill

When Jack and Jill began to get involved with sex, they felt it was their own business. They figured no one was affected but them, so what difference did it make to anyone else if they had sex or not. An unexpected pregnancy showed them how many people it made a difference to.

As you read each character sketch below, try to imagine that you are the person being described. How would you feel about Jack and Jill and their pregnancy?

Jack is seventeen, a junior in high school and a star athlete. He is a good student with plans to be a medical doctor. He's been worried for several weeks because his girlfriend Jill has missed two periods. He just found out that she is definitely pregnant.

Jack's mother is proud of her eldest son. She has always been pleased with his maturity and sense of responsibility. She likes his girlfriend. Jill even comes over sometimes when Jack isn't home just to talk to her. Jack just told his mom that Jill is three months pregnant.

Jack's father is a blue-collar worker who has been saving for years to send his son to medical school. He wants Jack to have a better chance in life than he had. Now his wife tells him that Jack's girlfriend is pregnant.

Jill is a sophomore, almost sixteen, who has been going with Jack for a year. She is in the drama club and thinks she has a good chance of getting the lead part in the spring play. But the doctor told her yesterday that she is expecting a baby in June.

Jill's mother has been upset with her youngest daughter lately because she spends too much time with Jack. Jill's grades have never been good, and this isn't helping. She is also sad because Jill doesn't tell her everything the way she once did. This morning, though, Jill told her mom that she is three months pregnant.

Jill's dad always looks forward to the weekends his "little girl" spends with him. He is also beginning to like Jack, the young man she's been seeing. Today his ex-wife called him with the news: His little girl is pregnant.

Jill's older sister lives in a neighboring state. She is married and has two adopted children. Jill has always confided in her, but she didn't tell her she was sexually involved with Jack. Today her mother phoned with the news about the pregnancy.

Jack's little brother, who is ten, idolizes Jack. Jack takes him places, plays ball with him, and lets him listen to his iPod. He has always wanted to be just like Jack in everything. Today he saw his mother crying and was told about Jill.

Jill's grandmother is very active in her parish and goes to prayer meetings every week. She took care of Jill when she was little, and Jill has always been her darling. When she heard about the pregnancy, Grandma vividly remembered the day she heard the same news about Jill's mother.

Jill's best friend was the very first person Jill told. The two girls have been friends since grade school and have always shared their "love lives" with each other. When they were freshmen they made a pact that they would both stay virgins until they got married. Now Jill cries every time they talk.

Jack's coach heard the news in the faculty room. It explained a lot about Jack's sloppy basketball season. The coach had noticed that Jack seemed distracted and preoccupied for the last several weeks. He didn't come to talk like he usually did. Now Coach wonders why Jack didn't tell him about this problem with Jill.

Jill's drama teacher thinks Jill is one of the most promising young actresses she's worked with. Even though Jill is just a sophomore, she picked the spring play with her in mind for the lead. She just now heard the rumors.

Jack's former girlfriend always liked being with Jack because he was so much fun and yet so respectful of her old-fashioned values. She still likes him as a friend, but she doesn't get to talk to him very often since he's been going with Jill. She just found out about the pregnancy.

Jack's cousin was married last year to a junior girl he got pregnant. Things aren't going well for him. His job pays just above minimum wage, he's always fighting with his young wife, and the baby is sick and fussy much of the time. Now he hears about Jack.

Jill's friend Bob has liked Jill since eighth grade. He talks to her in study hall almost every day, but he never asks her out because he is afraid she'd turn him down. He knows, though, that Jill is the kind of girl he wants to marry some day. He just heard the rumors.

God has known and loved both Jack and Jill since the first moment they were created. God watched them mature and saw them getting deeply involved in a relationship they really think is love. Now there is a little person growing in Jill's body. If you were God, how would you feel about Jack and Jill? What would you want them to know? What would you want them to do?

The announcement of a pregnancy in a family ought to be a wonderful, exciting event for everyone involved. If it were a few years later, and if Jack and Jill were happily married, the news that they were expecting a baby would be received with much joy and anticipation.

Look back over the characters listed above and think about how different each person would feel if Jack and Jill were a young, married couple expecting the birth of their first child.

Dear Mom[4]

A sample of these imaginative letters from a baby inside the mother's womb helps you to get an idea of a baby's further development during its first nine months of existence.

Dear Mom,

It's hard for me to remember in this first month that you don't even know I'm here yet. My arms, legs, and head are forming already. I can move and close my mouth and even swallow. I get all my nourishment through the umbilical cord that attaches me to you, but I'm starting to develop my own circulation system that's separate from yours. I'm already as big as a pea.

LOVE,
YOUR BABY—FIRST MONTH

Dear Mom,

You know what? I'm a boy! That became evident during this my third month. My fingers and toes are distinct now, too; they even have soft nails. There are twenty little buds in my mouth for baby teeth, and my brain is starting to send signals telling me where and how to move. By the end of this month I'll be the size of a lemon.

LOVE,
YOUR LITTLE BOY—THIRD MONTH

Dear Mom,

I'm twelve inches already, and when I stretch and move around you probably think I'm kicking you. I look almost like a miniature baby, but you'd think I was ugly if you saw me. My skin is all wrinkled and red and covered with fine soft hair. By the end of this month I'll be the size of a small squash. Tell Dad to put his hand on your stomach so I can give him a friendly kick.

LOVE,
YOUR GROWING BOY—SIXTH MONTH

Dear Mom,

Okay, world, here I come! I'm going to be in your arms soon, Mom. My face, head, and body have filled out, and I'm ready for my journey to the outside world. I'm as big as a small watermelon, but I don't have to tell you that, do I? I weigh seven pounds, and I'm gaining a half of a pound a week. Thanks, Mom, for taking care of me so well all these months. It sure has been a nice comfortable world for me to live in. Do you think I'll like your big world as much as I like this little one? Tell Dad I'll be with you both in a couple of weeks.

LOVE,
YOUR SON—NINTH MONTH

Pregnancy is a serious responsibility. The baby developing within its mother's body needs very special care and protection. The first two months, before the parents even know about the pregnancy, are the most critical for the baby's development. Things that the mother does, or doesn't do, can have a permanent effect on the physical, mental, and emotional health of her unborn child.

There is a good chance that someone reading this book is already sexually active. If you are currently in a relationship that includes sexual intercourse, or if you have had any kind of intimate sexual contact during the past two or three months, there is at least a one-in-ten chance that you or your girlfriend is pregnant right now. If so, your responsibility as parents has already begun. First of all, this means that you or your girlfriend must immediately seek medical attention under the care of an OB/GYN who will suggest a strict prenatal regimen of diet, rest, and exercise.

Personal Journal

- Describe in your own words the miracle of pregnancy.
- How would the pregnancy of one of the following people affect you: you/your girlfriend now? a sibling? a close friend? you and your spouse after you are married?

- Write several questions you have about pregnancy or childbirth. Ask an adult you trust to help you answer them.

6

NO EASY CHOICES: ADOPTION, TEEN MARRIAGE, TEEN PARENTING, ABORTION

Every year nearly one million teenagers in the United States become pregnant. An unplanned pregnancy presents the teenage couple with one of the most serious choices of their lives. Whether they are ready to do so or not, they are forced into making a profoundly important moral decision.

Hopefully most of you who are reading this book will never find yourself in that kind of crisis position. But even if you don't, it is very likely that you may have to help a friend or relative decide what to do about a problem pregnancy. The material in this chapter looks realistically at the four alternatives an unmarried pregnant teen is faced with: adoption, teen marriage, single parenting, and abortion.

None of the four options is easy. None of them is without problems. None of them presents itself as the single right answer for every teenager in every pregnancy situation. All of the options are legal, but one of them, abortion, is a serious moral evil. All of the options will have long-range consequences for everyone involved—the teen mother and father, their families and friends, and especially the unborn child.

Note to Parents

Whether or not the teens reading this book will ever have to face an unmarried pregnancy situation personally, they are likely to have a relative or friend who has to decide what to do about a problem pregnancy. This chapter examines the four options for handling teen pregnancy: adoption, marriage, single parenting, and abortion. Though none of the four options is illegal, each is fraught with many difficulties. And, one of the options—abortion—is a serious moral evil. The activities in this chapter attempt to provide all sides of these options, with special emphasis placed on the positive choice of adoption.

Decision-Making Process

Just as there are many actors (girl, boy, parents, friends, siblings, grandparents, etc.) involved in a teenage pregnancy, there are many factors that influence a teenager facing a crisis pregnancy. Each factor contributes a different perspective, offers a different solution. It helps to have a process for looking at the complexities of such a major problem. In order to decide well, a person needs to prayerfully and thoughtfully reflect on each of the following factors. The thinking should be done before a crisis arises.

- What are the options? What are all the possible solutions to the problem?
- What facts are needed in order to make an informed decision? These may include several types of information—medical, sociological, economic, and moral, among others.
- Another aspect involves the law. Civil law may have some impact on possible solutions. Church law, and most important, God's law must be taken into account, so we need to consider what our faith tells us about the situation.
- Yet another major consideration is who will be affected by the consequences of the decision? Who has rights and responsibilities in this particular situation?

Those with experience may offer insights that will be helpful. It is worthwhile to consult adults who you believe share your same values or the values of your family and religion. Your religious leaders fit in this category. Also, it is worthwhile to talk with people who have made such a decision and people who have faced the consequences of the decision.

Finally, it is most important to seek out God in prayer as you honestly consider the values, morals, and convictions taught by the Church and held by you.

Adoption: A True Love Option

One option in a teen pregnancy is adoption, something that many pregnant teens today do not consider. If you are ever in a situation where you or someone you love has to make a decision about a crisis pregnancy, you should definitely consider adoption as one of your alternatives. In many cases adoption may be the very best option both for the teen parents and for the unborn child.

Each year there are nearly two million couples listed with adoption agencies in the United States, all hoping for a baby to adopt. Usually they have to wait many years before an adoptable baby becomes available.

Unfortunately, only 1–3 out of 100 teen pregnancies ends up with a baby who is put up for adoption. The graph below indicates the results of unplanned teen pregnancies and adoptions for a recent year:

Births	
●	Unmarried mother
✦	Married mother (baby conceived before marriage)
✝	Married mother (baby conceived after marriage)

Abortions & Miscarriages	
✗	Abortions
❑	Miscarriages

21%	●	●	●	●	●	●	●	●	●		1% Adoptions
	●	●	●	●	●	●	●	●	●	●	
10%	✦	✦	✦	✦	✦	✦	✦	✦	●	●	
17%	✝	✝	✝	✝	✝	✝	✝	✝	✦	✦	
	✗	✝	✝	✝	✝	✝	✝	✝	✝	✝	
	✗	✗	✗	✗	✗	✗	✗	✗	✗	✗	
38%	✗	✗	✗	✗	✗	✗	✗	✗	✗	✗	
	✗	✗	✗	✗	✗	✗	✗	✗	✗	✗	
	❑	❑	❑	✗	✗	✗	✗	✗	✗	✗	
13%	❑	❑	❑	❑	❑	❑	❑	❑	❑	❑	

Out of 100 unmarried pregnant teens:

- 37 chose to have their baby aborted
- 17 had a miscarriage
- 12 married the baby's father before the baby was born
- 31 raised the baby themselves in their parents' home
- 3 allowed the baby to be adopted by a married couple able to provide a loving home for him/her

Melissa's Journal

This journal was written by Melissa, a seventeen-year-old pregnant junior who chose the adoption option. The journal covers the ten months from the time when Melissa discovered she was pregnant until the formal adoption proceedings were completed. Though the journal is an actual account of Melissa's pregnancy, all the names in the journal are fictitious.

December

Today is my seventeenth birthday. I couldn't enjoy the family party at all. My cards said all those typical things—how loved a daughter I was, what a joy it is to have a niece like me. Deep inside I'd like to believe them. But there is another feeling in there. It's a sick, scary feeling that I'm too afraid to even write about for fear it will come true.

It seems the only time I allow myself to think about my problem is when I'm writing in this journal. I feel like I'm losing control. I still can't say that word—that word that probably describes me right now. I've got to talk to Tom—soon. I don't think he'll be angry, or that he'll run. I'm lucky in that way, I guess. Lucky? My sense of humor surprises me.

I'm going to tell Tom tomorrow when he takes me out to dinner. All I want is to be out of this mess.

Well, it went okay (my date with Tom, that is). We've had so many personal conversations in the past eight months. But tonight was the real test. I wonder why it was that we always talked about so many other things except for sex, and when we did talk about it, we sure didn't get it quite clear. Well, things are pretty clear now. Tom told me to let him know if there are any changes. I don't know what he's hoping for. I'm positive that this is real.

January

I know I have to face up to things, but I just can't. Maybe it would be easier if we both didn't exist. This life inside me deserves better than me. It would be easier on everyone if I just . . . Oh, God! The only thing that scares me more than being pregnant is hearing myself talk that way. I can handle it, somehow. We can! Tom and I and God.

I'm a statistic now. Maybe there's a category they can stuff me under to keep me safe. Anyway, I'm glad Tom went to the doctor with me.

Tom and I had another long talk tonight. I wish we were as certain about our solution as we are about our problem. I really wish I could talk to my mom—just as a person instead of a daughter. What kind of daughter am I anyway? I feel awful. I'm all alone at home, and I'm very scared.

February

I can't write much because I'm all cried out. Tom and I just spent several hours talking and crying with my mom. She hugged me and told me she loves me. She even hugged Tom. She told us both that we would all make it and that somehow we can pull together to survive.

The weekend went pretty well, under the circumstances. Things aren't all warm and fuzzy at home though. I'm glad I know that my mom loves me. I just hope she realizes that I love her too. I'm beginning to see that this pregnancy affects her almost as much as it does me.

March

Mom and I have been talking a lot about adoption. It'll be hard, but Mom keeps telling me I have a lot of inner strength. It just seems like the best thing. I'm adopted, and I feel if my birth mother could do it, so can I. I just have to keep remembering that this pregnancy won't last forever.

Another argument with Tom, but at least we're still communicating. He wants to get married, but I'm planning on college. Adoption seems like the best answer for me and the baby. It's so clear to me now. Maybe it will be more difficult later on, but right now that's what I'm holding on to.

I had an appointment with Catholic Social Services today. I met Nan, the most concerned social worker in the world. I'll be seeing her every few weeks to check up on things. She's the one who will handle all the adoption stuff, and she'll speak for me when the service picks an adoptive couple. I think I can trust her.

April

I gave a talk in my confirmation class tonight. I was afraid when the director first asked me, but I'm glad she encouraged me to do it. She said that the Melissa she knew would be speaking from her heart and that was what the kids needed to hear. I just told everyone that we all make mistakes, but the Christian thing to do is to correct the mistake. I told them they should all look at their lives now and see if anything needs changing, not wait, like I did, until real trouble happens.

May

I'm conscious of the baby all the time now. I'm still scared, but kind of excited too about what's happening in there. I'm so glad Tom and I both agreed right at the beginning that abortion was not the right answer. I can handle this. I can feel myself growing more every day—and that's not meant to be a pun. Tom isn't saying much, but I know he would still like to get married and have us all be together.

June

Graduation at last. My friends have been terrific for me, but I'm still glad school is over. I feel like the Goodyear blimp. I'm uncomfortable, both physically and emotionally. I don't think Tom is aware of this at all. My mom is though. I wish she didn't have to go through all this. I'm starting childbirth classes next week.

I've started having second thoughts about the adoption. It seems like I'd be abandoning my very own baby.

I talked to Nan about my adoption fears. She is such a good counselor. I always feel like she's soaking in every syllable I say. Anyway, she reminded me that there is more than one way to abandon a baby. I know what she meant. If I spend the time I want to spend on college and a career, I won't really have time to give the baby enough attention.

July

It's hot, and I want this over with soon! I'm getting restless. The doctor told me it'll be a few days.

Well, he's here. My very own son. I'm going to call him Jason. It's wonderful to hold him. I feel I'm just keeping him for a while, though, till I give him to parents who can take care of him much better than I can. They can't love him more than I do though. My mom was a fantastic coach. I really couldn't have come through this so well without her.

I feel the strongest I've ever felt in my life. I am in control, and I'm proud of me. We had a little blessing service in the hospital before I left today. My family and friends came, and we blessed Jason and sort of said goodbye to him. It was a beautiful ceremony—not a dry eye there. Tom and I cried the most.

It's good to be home.

September

I met Megan and David today. What a wonderful couple. It felt so good to hear their joy and excitement about a child they couldn't physically have themselves. I know that's how my parents must have felt when they got me. I've made a great difference in their lives, and now, in another way, I'm going to make a wonderful difference in Meg and Dave's lives.

My mom and I went to court today to finalize the decision, and I came home feeling all right, literally. I'm sad, but my decision for adoption feels right. I know that Jason will grow up to be a happy little boy with his new parents.

Two years later

Today my Mom's friend Kieran called and asked me if I'd be willing to put excerpts from my journal in a book she's writing for teens. It sounds like a real opportunity. I learned so much through that experience, and I'd like to help other kids avoid making the mistakes Tom and I made.

I'm a freshman in college now and loving it. I'm not seeing Tom anymore, although we do keep in touch. We don't talk about Jason at all, but I'm sure he's on Tom's mind as he is on mine. My mom and I have grown closer and talk often about the changes in both of us since Jason's brief stay in our lives.

My decision couldn't have been a better one—both in the outcome and in the process I went through to reach it. I was too young for all of it, yet God helped me grow enough to handle it. And now I feel there's nothing I can't do!

When I look back I realize that the whole ordeal wasn't even a year of my life. What's that compared to Jason's whole future!

The day before the adoption papers were signed, Melissa, Tom, and Melissa's mother wrote letters to Jason. These are actual contents of those letters, which will be kept in Jason's file until his adoptive parents decide he is old enough to understand them.

Dear Jason,

You are my very first grandchild and will hold a special place in my heart always. Your mother is my only child. She too is adopted and entered my life at Christmas time when she was only three weeks old.

During the months Melissa carried you, everyone was touched by her reverence for your life and by her courage. She was only 17, but every decision and choice she made centered upon you. In choosing life for you, she became a model of hope and grace for other young women facing a similar decision. She wanted you to be born.

The two of you were cared for and loved by our family and close friends. We believed that, regardless of circumstances, all life comes from God's love, and is good!

Yours was a beautiful birth. You were born into gentleness and placed immediately in your mother's arms. She had asked for quiet voices and soft lights in the delivery room because she didn't want you startled or frightened. From those first few moments there was a special peacefulness and contentment in you.

Melissa nurtured you and cared for you in the few days you shared together, knowing that she would learn to love you and that separating from you would be even harder. She wanted to be sure you would know the security of a loving touch right from the start.

Tomorrow we must let you go toward your future with your adoptive parents. Melissa made this choice for you because she does love you. She hopes you will know the happiness of a more complete family love than she would be able to provide for you now. We are confident that you will be loved and that you will bring love to your new family.

There is painful grief in letting go, but I trust that the One who sent you into our lives will be with you and guide you toward the fullness of your manhood. You are precious to us and to him.

I love you, Jason!
Grandma

Dear Jason,

It seems kinda funny writing you this letter. Just three hours ago I was holding you in my arms, trying to explain to you why Melissa and I decided to give you up for adoption. You just stared up into my face as if you understood everything I said.

Our decision was probably the hardest thing I've ever done. I love you more than anything. We both do. I wish things were different—that Melissa and I were older, or felt more secure about marriage. As much as we hated to think about losing you, we made our decision out of great love for you. We would have kept you if there was any way we could have given you the life we knew you deserved. But we had to do what we felt was best for you.

From the first time I saw you, a few minutes after your birth, I was so proud of you. I knew at that moment that you were special. I am going to miss a lot of things about you—those funny faces you make, your big blue eyes, those ever so gentle moans and groans. But most of all I'm going to miss being able to share our lives together. I hope you can understand that we really do love you a lot.

I'm sure there will come a day when I will question whether what I did was right, but right now I am sure that it is. As much as it hurts, I believe it is the best thing to do.

I'm going to miss you very much. I'll always be thinking about you and praying for you. I hope you live a wonderful and happy life with your adopted parents.

I love you.
Your father,
Tom

Dear Jason,

You are such a special part of my life. I will always remember the time we spent together, even before you entered this world! You and I went everywhere together! We went to school, we celebrated Christmas, we shared secrets in the middle of the night, and we were even confirmed together by the bishop! Whenever I felt sad or lonely, you gave me a feeling of strength to help me go on. Of course you did your share of poking, too!

God took such good care of you and me. He sent special people who loved us and helped us understand His love and gentleness. I really did feel God's love when I saw your face for the first time. I had waited for that day for a long time!

Before we left the hospital, my family and friends gathered to bless you. Then a wonderful woman took you to her home until the adoption would be settled. I missed you very much and came to visit you with your grandmother and your father. You were such a beautiful baby, always so content and happy.

I thought about you all the time. I knew that I wanted to do the best thing for you, no matter what that was. It took two months before I finally decided to let you be adopted. This was hard for me, and for your father, but we know it's the best way to show you that we love you.

I will always remember you, both with a smile and with a tear. I will see you in everything that is beautiful in this world. I will remember how strong you made me feel when I was carrying you. I learned from you that life is very precious, and that you and I are precious in God's eyes. I know God will watch over us and will keep us together, no matter where we are.

I love you, Jason!
Your birth mother,
Melissa

Teenage Marriage: Happily Ever After?

When your grandparents were young, the solution to a pregnancy outside of marriage was almost always to get married. Both families would exert strong pressure on the couple to get married before the baby was born. It was called a "shot-gun wedding."

Today only about 12 percent of teen girls who get pregnant choose to marry. Unlike generations past, very few parents today would advise marriage as a good solution. The odds against a teen marriage working are very strong. The circumstances of most young people in today's complex world just do not make marriage advisable.

Let's look at a few couples who will help illustrate the problems facing teenagers who might be considering marriage. In each case the girl is pregnant and each couple is thinking about getting married. What would you advise them to do?

- Mark and Jan have been friends for two years and have been dating for six months. They are both involved in sports and usually spend their time together doing things like playing tennis or swimming. They're both juniors and have vague plans for college, especially if they can get athletic scholarships. They had sex only a few times, and he always thought he was protected. Now Jan is pregnant and they are considering marriage.
- Dave and Carol met at a party six months ago. She's fifteen and he's seventeen. They go to different schools and neither is a very good student. They had sex the first night they went out and have done it often since then, usually in his car. She uses the pill whenever she can find some in her older sister's drawer. They've never been to each other's homes or met each other's families. Now Carol is pregnant and wondering if she should marry Dave.
- Rick and Cindy have been friends since grade school and have dated off and on since they were freshmen. Now they are seniors and quite mature for their age. He's assistant manager at a retail store, and she has a weekend job at a restaurant. They fight a lot because he goes out with other girls. They usually have sex when they are making up after a fight. They

never use contraceptives, but he tries to withdraw when he thinks about it. Cindy is pregnant and thinking about marriage.

- Prom night was Tony and Linda's first date. Like most of their friends, they chipped in for a hotel suite after prom. Lots of couples were taking turns using the bedroom for sex. Linda was afraid at first, but the more she had to drink the more she wanted to do it. The day after the prom they were both pretty embarrassed, and he felt really guilty about what they had done. They've dated a few times since then, but they only had sex on prom night. Linda knows now that she is pregnant. Should she marry Tony?
- Shawn and Kristin started going out together the summer after their sophomore year and have dated for two years now. They both had strong moral convictions against premarital sex, and he has even thought seriously about becoming a priest. Then one day they were at his house, his parents weren't home, and one thing just led to another. They promised God and each other that they wouldn't do it again, but whenever they are alone at her house or his, they just can't seem to help it. Now Kristin is pregnant. Shawn thinks the right thing to do is marry her.
- Jim and Marcia are very much in love and have talked of marriage for a long time. Jim already works at his father's auto repair business, and he plans to get a vocational degree in mechanics and business after high school. Marcia wants to be a hair stylist. They have sex often, but try to do it only during her safe time. Her parents don't like Jim or his family and have been trying for months to get them to break up. They don't know yet that they are planning to marry soon.
- Brett has never loved any girl as much as he loves Kathy, but sometimes she finds his affection a little too much to handle. He gave up drinking for her, and since they've been going together he's stopped cutting school so often. She likes him very much, but she doesn't like the feeling that he owns her. He's been all the more possessive since they started

having sex. Now that she's pregnant, he wants to marry her so he can keep her forever.

- This is the first serious relationship for Matt, but Joni's been around. Most of her other flings were just short-term experiences with guys she met at parties. The last time she was pregnant she had an abortion. He says he knows all about her past history. But he loves her, will forgive her for all, and marry her. He says she's really different now that she's been going out with him. His parents didn't like her even before they found out she was pregnant.

Teen Parenting: A Full-Time Responsibility

Many unmarried teens who are faced with a crisis pregnancy decide to keep and raise the baby themselves. However, in most cases the baby is cared for in the home of the teenage mother and her family. The baby's father usually plays little or no role in raising the child, though in some states the father is legally responsible to pay child support. Once in a great while the baby's father and his family assume full care of the baby.

It's important as you strengthen your resolve not to get involved sexually as a teenager to have a realistic idea of how your whole life would be changed if you were to become a teen parent.

All the teens described and quoted below speak from personal experience.

> Having a baby has changed my life a lot. I love my daughter very much, but I'm not as free as I used to be. Now when I want to go somewhere, I can't just pick up and go. I have to get my baby ready too.
>
> Judy—16

> I told Jeannie before the baby was born that I would help her as much as I could. But she never thinks I do enough. She expects me to babysit two or three nights a week, and she always wants money for this and money for that. We hardly ever have time for each other anymore.
>
> Tom—18

I'm not really raising her myself. It's more like my mom who raises her, and I just come to visit. I go to school and I have a job, so I'm gone most of the time. She even calls my mom "Mama," which I don't like very much.

Brenda—16

My mother is always telling me what to do. She keeps treating me as though I don't know how to take care of a baby. I want to live in my own place, but it takes all the money I can scrape together just to buy the things Matthew needs.

Cathy—19

The thing that is hardest is my friends, or I should say former friends. Before the baby was born they were real nice, but since then they never call or come over. Even if they do call, I usually can't go out because there isn't anyone to take care of Stevie.

Darla—15

My biggest problem is being lonely. When I moved into the apartment I thought Eric would move in with me, but he started dating other girls and doesn't even come over anymore to see Gina. I'm just stuck here by myself with a screaming baby day after day.

Mary Jo—18

It's hard because I really do love my baby daughter. It's just that I get so upset and tired. I never dreamed a baby could be so much work and take so much time. I want to be a good father, but sometimes I'm just crabby and mean like my father always was.

Dan—18

My ex-boyfriend doesn't pay any child support, so most of the burden falls on my folks. I feel embarrassed about that, because they have enough trouble supporting their own children. My mom wants me to date and meet other guys, but not too much because she really doesn't want to babysit very often.

TANYA—17

Abortion: Morality vs. Legality

The following letter was written by an eighteen-year-old senior in a Catholic high school. The letter shows what can happen when Catholic teens like Sandy, Darla, Amy, and Rick experience an unplanned pregnancy. They find themselves considering the possibility of abortion and are brought face to face with the reality that abortion is both a legal right and a moral evil.

Letter From Sandy

My best friend Darla is pregnant. She immediately decided to have an abortion because she and her boyfriend Rick had already determined that is what they would do if it ever happened. When she told me and our two other friends about the pregnancy, we almost expected it because they were so irresponsible. But we were all surprised that she would even think of killing it. One of my friends immediately lashed out at her and went off on the immorality of abortion. Darla felt backed into a corner and defended herself.

My other friend, Amy, said that she didn't agree with Darla's decision, but she would go with her to the abortion clinic because Darla is her friend. She felt it wouldn't be immoral for her, because she had no part in the decision itself. After two days Amy changed her mind and took back the offer to go with her. Darla was completely abandoned except for me. I felt that she was doing the wrong thing too. But I decided that enough people were telling her that it was wrong—what she really needed was support.

I'm a trained peer counselor, so I used my peer counseling skills. But after a while I discovered that it wasn't enough for me to just be the "brick wall" that she bounced things off of. I told her how I felt, and she made me feel guilty for "abandoning" her. I felt bad and told her later that I had changed my mind and that I did understand why she felt she had to have the abortion. She began to trust me more.

Now I'm acting as her peer counselor again—and it's eating away at my insides. I feel trapped by two walls that are both closing in on me.

Sandy

As an individual Catholic Christian and as an American citizen, you must take a personal stance on the abortion question. This will require much serious prayer and reflection on your part. It will require that you study what the Church teaches and what the government holds regarding this question. It is good to do the praying and thinking now, before you and/or someone you love are thrown into a crisis situation.

The first step in understanding the complex issue of abortion is to differentiate between the legal question and the moral question. The legal question asks: Does a woman have the legal right to choose abortion? The moral question asks: Is it morally right for a woman to choose abortion? The complexity of the problem stems from the fact that the two questions are intertwined in people's minds, and that few people answer either with a straight yes or no answer.

The Legal Question

Since 1973, the federal government has answered the legal question with an almost unqualified yes—yes, a woman has the legal right to choose abortion. In the Roe v. Wade decision, the United States Supreme Court ruled that the Fourteenth Amendment to the United States Constitution provided the fundamental right for women to obtain abortions. According to this ruling the woman's right to control her own body takes precedence over all other considerations. The unborn child is not considered a legal person and has no rights under the law.

Two separate Supreme Court Cases in 1989 (Webster) and 1992 (Planned Parenthood v. Casey) gave individual states more latitude in qualifying or restricting the right to an abortion. Some states restrict abortion to the first three months of pregnancy; some require parental notice or consent; some allow abortion only if the mother's life is in danger; and so forth.

In April 2007 the United States Supreme Court upheld by a vote of 5–4 the Federal Partial-Birth Abortion Ban Act of 2003 in Gonzales v. Carhart. Cardinal Justin Rigali, the Chairman of Pro-Life Activities for the United States Conference of Catholic Bishops, with cautious optimism said:

> The Court's decision does not affect the legal status of the great majority of abortions, and does not reverse past decisions claiming to find a right to abortion in the Constitution. However, it provides

> reasons for renewed hope and renewed effort on the part of pro-life Americans. The Court is taking a clearer and more unobstructed look at the tragic reality of abortion, and speaking about that reality more candidly, than it has in many years.[5]

Abortion law and its interpretation is a matter of constant debate by United States citizens as well as by federal and state legislatures and courts. It is important for thinking Catholics to remember that the fact that a woman has the legal right to choose abortion does not make it morally right for her to do so.

The Moral Question

From a moral perspective, the rightness or wrongness of abortion depends largely on whether the unborn is a distinct human being. If what is present in the womb were simply "fetal tissue," abortion would be as morally neutral as having one's appendix removed. But since the fetus is a human life, abortion is as morally serious as killing a baby.

Because the fetus is a human life, the answer the Catholic Church gives to the moral question is an unqualified no. It is not morally right for a woman to choose to have an abortion. The Church teaches that:

> Human life must be respected and protected absolutely from the moment of conception. From the first moment of existence, a human being must be recognized as having the rights of a person—among which is the inviolable right of every innocent being to life.
>
> (CATECHISM OF THE CATHOLIC CHURCH, 2270)

The Church teaches that the rights of this unborn child are to be protected in the same way any human life is protected. Therefore, it cannot be right for a woman to choose an abortion; abortion is a serious moral evil.

> . . . Direct abortion, that is abortion willed as an end or as a means, always constitutes a grave moral disorder, since it is the deliberate killing of an innocent human being. This doctrine is based upon the natural law and the written Word of God, is transmitted by

> the Church's Tradition and taught by the ordinary and universal Magisterium.
>
> No circumstance, no purpose, no law whatsoever can ever make licit an act which is intrinsically illicit, since it is contrary to the law of God which is written in every human heart, knowable by reason itself, and proclaimed by the Church.[6]

Unfortunately, not everyone accepts this clear stance on the immorality of abortion. Some people hold that there is nothing morally wrong with abortion. They see abortion as an alternate method of birth control, even as a necessary means of population control.

The social norm (what "everybody says") regarding abortion falls someplace between the two extreme positions. Most people say that they consider abortion to be wrong, but feel there are some "exceptional cases" in which it might be admissible—incest, rape, a handicapped or retarded unborn child, or a life-threatening condition of the mother. However, of the thousands of abortions performed in the United States each day, less than two percent come within the "exceptional case" category. The vast majority of abortions (more than 98 percent) are chosen for other reasons: the age of the mother; pressure from the baby's father; embarrassment, shame, and fear; financial problems, career goals, and job security; preferred sex of the baby; or even personal convenience.

The civil law that makes abortion legal says only that the abortion decision is to be left up to the woman; it does not make it right for her to choose abortion. God's law comes before civil law. The fifth commandment clearly states: "Thou shall not kill." Abortion destroys the life of an unborn child and is, therefore, a sin against the law of God.

Post-Abortion Syndrome

There is a real possibility that someone reading this book has already had an abortion or knows someone who has. If so, you realize that abortion is not an easy way out. Many people who have been involved in an abortion suffer aftereffects of severe emotional, psychological, and spiritual problems. The first reaction to having an abortion may be relief, but that relief is often followed—sooner or later—by a sense of deep guilt and profound grief over the loss of the child.

Many women who have had an abortion suffer from what is called post-abortion syndrome. They experience deep feelings of loss. They are filled with fear, anxiety, guilt, and remorse. They suffer feelings of low self-esteem, alienation, and loneliness. Because the abortion is usually secret, all of this spiritual pain is kept inside, sometimes leading to severe depression and even suicide.

The problems connected with post-abortion syndrome do not go away by themselves. If they are not dealt with, they remain beneath the surface of the person's consciousness and affect every aspect of life, especially the person's feelings about love and sexuality.

Anyone reading this book who has been involved in an abortion in any way should seek out professional and spiritual counseling. School counselors, your parish ministers, or diocesan outreach offices like Family Life, can direct you to persons and programs that provide healing, counseling, prayer, and the sacrament of reconciliation for those suffering from the aftereffects of an abortion.

Personal Journal

- How would a pregnancy affect your life?
- To whom would you turn if you needed advice concerning a pregnancy?
- How would you feel about giving up a child for adoption? How would you feel about adopting a child?
- What would your life be like as a teen parent raising a child?
- Write a poem or reflection that captures your beliefs about life for the unborn.
- Imagine that you or your girlfriend have decided to give a child up for adoption. Write an imaginary letter to the child explaining your choice.

7

CONTRACEPTION: IS IT A SAFE CHOICE?

One of the biggest lies that has been perpetrated on teenagers is represented by the slogan "safe sex." Usually the message of safe sex is accompanied by a pitch for using a condom. Admittedly, condoms do offer some degree of protection against pregnancy, sexually transmitted diseases, and AIDS—but certainly not enough for you to risk your life and health over. As Dr. Teresa Crenshaw, a member of the U.S. Presidential AIDS Commission, put it,

> Saying that the use of condoms is "safe sex" is in fact playing Russian roulette. A lot of people will die in this dangerous game.

A few years ago, Dr. Crenshaw lectured at a World Congress on AIDS in Germany, attended by the top doctors and medical professionals of the world. Dr. Crenshaw relates this conversation:

> I asked them this question: If they themselves had available the sexual partner of their dreams, and knew that that person carried the AIDS virus, would they have sex, depending on a condom for protection?
>
> In a room of more than a thousand people, no one raised their hand. After a long delay, one timid hand surfaced in the back of the room.
>
> I told them that it was irresponsible to give advice to others that they would not follow themselves.
>
> The point is, putting a mere balloon between a healthy body and a deadly disease is not safe.[7]

This chapter focuses on various forms of contraception, their health risks and their effectiveness for preventing pregnancy and sexually transmitted diseases. This material is based on the Catholic teaching that sexual intercourse is only to be practiced within marriage, and therefore, the only form of birth control that is moral outside of marriage is abstinence. This chapter also seeks to provide a dissenting voice to the myth that "safe sex" outside of marriage is even possible.

Note to Parents

Today's teens grow up on the myth that has come to be known as "safe sex." A contention of the safe sex myth is that teenagers who use a condom to prevent sexually transmitted disease and pregnancy are acting responsibly. Besides contradicting the teaching of chastity, the safe sex myth does not take into account the fact that condoms are often unreliable due to human and product error and, even if used properly, have an unacceptable failure rate in the areas of both pregnancy and sexually transmitted disease. This chapter helps teens to discover for themselves the fallacy of the "safe sex" myth.

Isn't Everybody Doing It?

"Everybody's having sex." That's what a good many teenagers think, due mainly to the messages they receive from the media, and to a lesser degree the bravado of some of their peers.

In fact, recent studies show that 50 percent of high school aged teens are not sexually active, and recent studies show this number moving closer to 60 percent. Moreover, statistics show that young people who are not sexually active tend to have many other positives going for them, including:

- They tend to have clear goals and definite future plans.
- They rate high in self-esteem and self-confidence.
- They are likely to come from good family structures with a strong moral and faith background.
- They have many friends of both sexes and a healthy sense of belonging.
- They tend to be serious about academics and involved in many school and Church activities.

- They have good leadership skills and show greater maturity and responsibility.
- They are less likely to be involved in alcohol and drugs.

On Taking Risks

There are obviously many risks associated with teenage sexuality. Before examining those risks specifically, familiarize yourself with risk-taking in general:

- Risk-taking is often a response to a dare from a peer. The challenge comes from wanting to prove oneself, to seem not afraid. Safety is often disregarded. This behavior often begins around the age of ten and, with some people, continues through adulthood.
- Those who encourage risky behavior in others may be at least partly motivated by anger, jealously, or dislike for the person.
- "Accidents" due to risk-taking may not really be accidents. Often an injury is a conscious or unconscious effort by the person to gain attention.

On the other hand, an adult-level response to risks includes all of the following steps:

- You try to discover all of the risks that might be involved in the situation.
- You look clearly at the probable and possible consequences connected with each risk.
- You consider how you might eliminate or decrease any of the negative possibilities.
- You weigh the hoped-for positive outcomes against the possible negative outcomes.
- You decide to act or not to act based on these considerations.
- You accept full responsibility for the outcomes of your choice whether they are positive or negative.

Risks Connected with Teenage Sex

As you review the following risks connected with teenage sexual activity, decide if it is a risk outweighed by one of the reasons teens give for having sex.

1. **AIDS, STDs** Any person who engages in sexual activity risks being infected or infecting the other person with a variety of diseases that are transmitted sexually. Reports from the Centers for Disease Control show that one in four sexually active teens will contract some form of sexually transmitted disease.
2. **Pregnancy** No contraceptive method is 100 percent effective, especially for teenagers. If semen comes in contact with the natural lubricants in or around the vagina, pregnancy is possible even if penetration does not occur. Some more recent statistics:

   - 43% of all unintended pregnancies occurred while using contraception.
   - 20% of teen girls who become sexually active become pregnant within the first month of sexual activity; 50% become pregnant within the first six months.
   - 85% of teen pregnancies are unintended.

3. **Pregnancy Panic** Even if pregnancy does not occur, a sexually active teenager lives with the constant fear of pregnancy. This state of anxiety is a serious risk to the teen's psychological and emotional health.
4. **Loss of Reputation** On one hand, many teens make fun of virginity and laugh at teens who haven't "done it" yet. On the other, teens freely use negative words (e.g., slut, stud) to label those who engage in casual sex. A teenager who becomes sexually active is putting his or her reputation on the line.
5. **Ruined Relationship, Break-Up** More often than not, premarital sex destroys the relationship it was intended to seal. When sexual intercourse takes place outside a committed marriage, it can very easily degenerate into exploitation.
6. **Conflict with Parents** Sex is one of the main sources of parent-teen conflict. Sexually active teens often find themselves resorting to lies, deception, evasiveness, and disobedience, all of which seriously damage the trust relationships they have built up with their parents.

7. **Sin, Guilt, Shame** No matter what their religious or family training, most young people have been taught that premarital sex is wrong and feel guilty when they do it. The Catholic Church teaches that fornication (sex between an unmarried man and unmarried woman) is an offense against the sixth commandment, "You shall not commit adultery." Persons who are sexually active before marriage risk carrying into their future marriages the feelings of sin, guilt, and shame that they have associated with sexual activity.
8. **Weakened Relationship with God** Involvement with premarital sex often drives a wedge between a teen and God. The sexually active teen usually senses the sinfulness of his or her actions and feels hypocritical about prayer and religious activities.
9. **Emotional Upheaval** Teenage sex can cause a wide range of intense emotions. Excitement, fear, hurt, suspicion, rejection, guilt, relief, anger, and regret follow one another in a roller coaster ride of highs and lows that is often psychologically dangerous. This risk is compounded by the use of mood-altering drugs, especially alcohol.
10. **Regret, Depression, Suicide** A heavy sexual relationship usually promises a teenager far more than it can deliver. The more the relationship seems like real love, the more the young person is likely to invest, and the deeper the pain and hurt if the relationship breaks up. The despair that follows a breakup is a leading cause of teen suicide. Suicide is the third leading cause of death for fifteen- to twenty-four-year-olds.
11. **Preoccupation, Distraction** A sexual relationship can completely absorb a young person's time, thoughts, dreams, and interests. Sexually active teens often neglect everything else—studies, sports, activities, families, friendships, and future plans.
12. **Loss of Self-Respect and Moral Standards** Many young people begin their teen years with high moral standards. Each lapse from these ideals leads more easily to another. Those who repeatedly act in a manner contrary to their own deepest values seriously diminish their sense of self-regard and can become morally callous.
13. **Foreclosure on Adolescence** Teens who get deeply involved in sex often miss out on the fun and excitement of learning gradually how to deal with sexuality. They lose the spontaneity and

freedom of being a teen and can find themselves abruptly facing decisions—about fidelity, pregnancy, marriage, and parenting—that they are not prepared to handle.

14. **Devaluing of Sexual Experience** A person who engages in casual sex loses the ability to use sexual intercourse as a sign of deep love and commitment. One can't move readily from fun sex with just anyone to loving, committed sex with one special person.
15. **Jeopardy to Future Married Happiness** Persons who engage in premarital sex tend to have less successful marriages. They are more likely than those who married as virgins to be disconnected, suspicious, and unfaithful in marriage.

How Safe Is Sex?

Sex outside of marriage is risky business. Though most people are aware of serious dangers like unwanted pregnancies or contracting AIDS or another STD, many teens, and adults, are convinced that the way to avoid them is to practice "safe sex," that is, to use contraceptives.

Contraception is another area in which there is a conflict between the moral teachings of the Church and the norms of society. The social community generally accepts the use of contraception by adults. The Catholic Church teaches that the use of artificial birth control is immoral, even for married couples.

However, even the social community is divided about the advisability of giving contraceptives to teens. Some adults feel that the way to protect teens from pregnancy and STDs is to make contraceptives easily available. Others believe that giving teenagers easy access to contraception increases the problems connected with teenage sexual activity. They point to statistics that show that the number of teen pregnancies goes up rather than down when teens are encouraged to use birth control.

To make a sound moral decision, you need to have a clear understanding of the teachings of the Church and the reasons for them. To counter the myth of "safe sex," you need an adequate understanding of the various methods of contraception and the limited degree of safety they provide.

The Catholic Church teaches that sexual intercourse is to be practiced only within marriage. Therefore the only form of birth control that is moral outside of marriage is abstinence.

The United States Catholic Bishops spoke directly to the issue of "safe sex" and contraceptive use for teenagers in "A Statement to Youth on School-Based Clinics." Imagine your bishop speaking directly to you.

> We do not believe that sexual activity among young people is inevitable. . . . We believe in your ability to choose another way of living—to learn the positive values of honesty, responsibility, promise-keeping, self-control, commitment, and respect for the other person that will help you to reserve your sexuality for marriage.
>
> We believe that the wide availability of contraceptives confirms teenagers in harmful sexual behavior. You are told to deal with your sexuality by using pills and devices, instead of learning about the beauty of God's plan and the responsible values that will help you to grow as a sexual person. The only 100 percent safe way to avoid an unwed pregnancy is to reserve sexual activity for marriage.

Society seems to encourage you to use contraception as a safe way to avoid the negative consequences of sexual activity. The Church tells you that sexual activity is dangerous with or without contraceptives and urges you to practice chastity. Whose advice will you listen to?

How Safe Are Contraceptives?

Not only is contraception not a safe way for teens to avoid risks, every type of contraception carries some risk in itself. These risks, too, should be taken into account as you make your personal decision regarding the choice between contraceptives and chastity.

For many teens, the very act of buying contraceptives or taking them into your possession in another way, is experienced as a deliberate transgression of their personal moral standards. Once you've taken this step, you can no longer convince yourself that sex is "accidental." A Catholic teen who uses contraceptives adds to the sin of premarital sex this additional transgression against the moral teachings of the Church. Most teens also feel guilty about the secrecy and duplicity required to hide contraceptives from their parents.

There is another serious moral risk involving contraceptives. Some methods of contraception prevent pregnancy after conception by destroying or dislodging an already fertilized ovum. If this happens, the method is really abortive, not contraceptive.

Most contraceptive methods, especially those used by women, require the advice and services of a doctor. All artificial birth control methods carry some short- and long-term health risks. For example:

The Pill Health risks include abnormal blood clotting and heart attacks, cancer, and gallbladder disease. Side effects include headaches, acne, weight gain, vaginal infections, and depression.

Norplant Expensive for insertion. Common side effects include headaches, acne, weight gain, nausea, nervousness, hair loss, mood swings, ovarian cysts, and scarring upon removal.

Depo-Provera Health risks are increasing headaches, dizziness, weight gain, loss in bone density, allergy, and ovarian cysts (and possibly cervical cancer, breast cancer, hemorrhaging, and fetal defect).

IUD Health risks include pelvic-inflammatory disease, permanent infertility, ectopic pregnancy, septic abortion, and death.

Condoms and Spermicides Side effects include irritation, allergy, urinary tract infection.

No contraceptive is 100 percent effective, and the effectiveness rate decreases when the user is young, inexperienced, and not under a doctor's supervision. Contraception can offer teens the delusion of protection and thus make them more vulnerable to pregnancy and STDs. The condom, for instance, has an effectiveness rating of 90 percent or higher when used by adults. When used by teens, the rating drops to 64 percent or less. Nor does the condom protect against disease. Among sexually active teenage girls, 30 percent whose male partner wore a condom contracted an STD within a six-month period.

The use or non-use of contraceptives can be a constant source of contention and conflict in a relationship. Many teens are reluctant to talk to their partner about contraception. They often do not know, and are afraid to ask, if their partner is using any form of protection.

Many teens simply assume that contraception is the other person's responsibility. "Don't worry, I'll take care of everything" is one of the famous lines used to pressure a reluctant date into having sex. Unfortunately "everything" doesn't usually include a baby.

The regular purchase and use of contraceptives can be bothersome and expensive. The pill, for instance, should be prescribed by a physician and then taken faithfully every day, not just the days one is planning to have sex. Condoms must be new, worn correctly, put on at the right time, and disposed of properly. Even Natural Family Planning, the Church-approved method for regulating the birth of children, takes months of careful monitoring by and communication between husband and wife before it is effective.

For the most part, teenagers do not have enough knowledge or maturity to assume the regular responsibility required to make contraception even minimally effective.

Safe sex is not safe.

The only guaranteed protection against the dangers connected with sex is to reserve sexual activity for marriage.

Personal Journal

- Is the "safe sex" message for teens really a myth? Explain your views.
- Why do members of your peer group have sex? What do you think of these reasons?
- What are the top three reasons for teens not to have sex?
- Do you believe that sexual activity among teenagers is inevitable? Why or why not?

8

SETTING LIMITS: A PERSONAL CHOICE

This chapter deals with the question of "How far is too far?" regarding sexual activity.

The question really involves another important decision that must already be made before you answer these questions. Have you decided to save sex until marriage or not?

If you have not decided to save sex until you have entered into the permanent commitment of marriage, there is little point to addressing the need for setting limits for sexual behavior before marriage.

However if your purpose is to keep from becoming involved sexually until marriage, the question of "how far is too far" has important relevance. It involves understanding the biological differences between male and female sexual response. It also involves understanding three types of relationships that may or may not include love and sex.

Note to Parents

This chapter helps teens come to a personal decision to refrain from premarital sex. To do this, teens explore three types of relationships: those where sex is a sign of real love, those where there is sex without real love, and those where there is real love without sex. In coming to understand these types of relationships, the teens are asked to develop a personal set of commandments regarding their sexual behavior and to learn various techniques to help them avoid temptations and say "no" to sex before marriage.

How Far Can We Go?

When teens ask the question, "How far can we go?" what they usually want to know is how far they can or should go toward sexual intercourse.

There is a natural progression in a relationship of sexual love. It moves from talking, to holding hands, to hugs and kisses, to passionate kissing, to sexual touching, to sexual intercourse.

People often call the development of romantic infatuation "falling in love." The movement from talking to sexual intercourse can happen gradually over many months, or it can happen, as it often does in the movies, in just a few days or hours.

How far you go toward sexual intercourse should really be answered as part of another natural progression, this one in a relationship of friendship/love. This progression involves a movement from being strangers, acquaintances, and companions to friendship, intimate friendship, and real love.

You probably have relationships at all stages of friendship/love, from the people you just know by name to those with whom you share your deepest secrets. It usually takes a long time, even years, for a friendship relationship to grow into real love.

The most complex type of relationship combines both progressions: romantic infatuation and friendship to love. Integrating the two in a developing love relationship is seldom easy because they move at such different paces. The question becomes: How do you learn to really love someone you are in love with?

Another factor that heavily influences a young person's response to the "how far" questions is his or her growth toward developing moral character. In the process of developing moral character, a person moves gradually from responding to situations only on the "child" level, which thinks only of fulfilling one's own needs and wants; to responding on the "pressure" level, in which choices are based on a desire to gain the approval of others—parents in the early childhood years, peers in the teen years; to responding on the "adult" level or the level of character, where decisions take into consideration respect for others, responsibility for the consequences of one's choices, a consideration of long-range life goals, and ultimately altruistic love for others.

The development of moral character corresponds to another important factor that must be considered in answering the "how far" question: how ready are you and your friend for parenthood? The long months and years during which true love relationships are developing should be paralleled by growth in the qualities and virtues that will be required for parenthood: qualities like responsibility, patience, caring, and tenderness.

Sexual Intercourse and Real Love—Three Contrasting Combinations

Sexual intercourse as a sign of real love

This is a simple description of married love. In marriage, two people make a lifetime commitment to love one another and then engage in sexual intercourse as a sign—a sacrament—of their love. When shared by a married couple, sexual intimacy is a source of mutual growth and understanding. Sex helps bond the couple into a unity that becomes the basis for creating a family and raising children.

The Catholic Church teaches that married love is a sacramental sign of God's love. This means that when a married couple has loving sex, the life of God is deepened within them, just as it is when they receive any of the other sacraments.

Sexual intercourse without real love

Unfortunately, many couples choose to have sexual intercourse even though they do not really love each other with the full commitment we have been describing. The social norms of society find sex more or less acceptable for couples who "love" each other even minimally. Love in this sense often equates more with infatuation than real love.

Some people choose to have sex before marriage in the hope that that sex will deepen their relationship. Although it may seem to be doing so for a time, uncommitted sex never leads to a true love relationship. It is much more likely that premature sex will destroy a relationship than deepen it. Premarital sex deceives a person or couple into thinking there is more love in the relationship than is really there. Sexual intimacy can be so wonderful and so exciting, especially in the beginning, that it is easily mistaken for real love. Choices and decisions based on that mistake can only lead to heartache.

Real love without sexual intercourse

A third possibility is real love without sexual intercourse. This is called celibate love. It is a clear and decisive choice not to express one's love through sexual intercourse or any of the foreplay that leads to sexual intercourse.

Two people may share deep personal and emotional intimacy. They may even experience intense sexual attraction. But they make a choice not to be sexually intimate. In many circumstances, this is the best way to express real love for someone.

There are some people who make a lifetime, vowed commitment to celibate love. They choose to be celibate in all of their relationships as a sign of their consecration to God and to God's people. Other people make a partial commitment to celibate love. Marriage, which is a commitment to sexual love in one exclusive relationship, implies that the couple also promises to be celibate in all of their other relationships.

Here are some other examples of real love without sexual intercourse: a man whose wife is ill or incapacitated chooses to be celibate out of love for her; the wife of a soldier chooses to be celibate until her husband comes home from war; a person with a homosexual orientation makes a moral and religious choice to maintain only celibate friendships; a person who has a contagious disease chooses to be celibate so as not to risk infecting the person he or she loves.

Finally, some people make a temporary commitment to celibate love. That is what we hope for each person reading this book.

Only a few of you will choose a lifetime commitment to celibacy. But God wants each of you to make the choice to abstain from sex until your marriage. We want you to realize that a commitment to abstinence-until-marriage is truly a love commitment. It is a profound way of showing your love for God, for yourself, for the person you may now be in love with, and for the person you may someday choose to marry.

The Brake Test

"How far can we go?" Use the following real-life situation to help answer this common question.

Dan and Stephanie are high school juniors. They have been friends for two years and have been dating for six months. Dan is a virgin and has made a decision not to have sex before marriage. Stephanie was involved sexually last year and is still recovering from a painful breakup. She has decided that she does not want to have sex again until after she is married.

Stephanie and Dan have to answer the how-far question every time they are alone together. How far is too far for them? How can they express their growing love and tenderness for one another without overstepping their personal moral boundaries? As young persons who really want to be celibate until marriage, where should they "put on the brakes?"

To give a realistic answer to the how-far question, Stephanie and Dan, and all young people in their position, need to understand a little biology.

The movement toward sexual intercourse is part of a powerful biological process that is not altogether within our conscious control. Love-play causes a physical reaction that gets increasingly difficult to contain the further you go with it.

For a while you are moving along on level ground. You are in control, and you can stop anytime you want. Then, often before you know it, you seem to be running straight downhill. It becomes increasingly difficult to put on the brakes. The biological drive for sexual fulfillment takes over and seems to overpower your consciously set limits, your personal values, your sense of responsibility, your respect for the other person, and your religious training.

There is a decided difference between the male and female response to sexual stimulation. It is a simple biological fact that males are sexually aroused more quickly than females. Females enjoy the warmth and coziness of prolonged hugging and kissing in and of themselves. Males often see these actions as an invitation to go further. A girl who is aware of this biological difference will be careful to avoid sexual teasing—stringing a boy along to the point where his sexual feelings are greatly aroused. A boy who is aware of the difference will realize that he has to let a girl know when he is becoming sexually aroused.

A couple who choose not to have sex before marriage have to set their brakes when they are both still on level ground. It can be very difficult to stop once either person has started running downhill.

If you are going to abstain from sex until marriage you will likely have to draw the line after simple hugs and kisses. Prolonged kissing and sexual touches can very quickly lead to sexual intercourse, which hopefully you have decided to avoid at this time. The signs of affection—hugs, kisses, touches—should help the relationship grow toward real love. Sexual intercourse before marriage has the opposite effect. Don't go "all the way" until your love goes all the way—to the sacramental love commitment of marriage. The following steps can help you to make and keep this important decision:

First, decide. Make a firm decision that you intend to refrain from sex until marriage. A half-hearted decision won't work.

Second, discuss your decision with your boyfriend or girlfriend. If you are not ready to discuss such an important matter, you certainly are not ready for sex.

Third, avoid temptation. Being in the wrong place at the wrong time with the wrong companions can quickly dissolve your decision to abstain from sex.

Fourth, avoid alcohol and other drugs. Being intoxicated inhibits your resolve and weakens your moral convictions.

Fifth, plan your dates. Know what you are going to do, where you're going to go. Keep busy with activities you both enjoy.

Sixth, pray. Remember that God loves you and wants you to be happy. Ask God's help every day. Talk to God about your temptations, your desires, your growing love for someone special. A powerful means of remaining celibate is to pray together for this special grace.

Love Language

One of the most exciting experiences in life is falling in love. And one of the biggest challenges is learning to use love language to communicate with the ones we love.

Listed below are some facts about love language:

1. **Love Language** is all of the spoken and non-spoken ways people say "I love you" to one another. It includes words and silence, looks and touches, actions and gifts, letters and songs, prayers and promises.
2. **Love Language** is true when it is tender, caring, responsible, thoughtful, compassionate, sensitive, honest, open, unselfish, considerate, controlled, respectful, and appropriate.
3. **Love Language** is false when it is used to exploit, dominate, pressure, hurt, arouse, tease, experiment, satisfy curiosity, take advantage of, prove a point, get back at, or get cheap thrills.
4. When **Love Language** is true, it brings life and growth, freedom and joy. When it is false it causes guilt, destruction, pain, tension, and grief.

5. **Love Language** can be deceptive. It can seem true when it is really false. It can change from being true to being false. It can mean different things to different people.
6. **Love Language** must be learned. Like any language, it takes practice and patience and persistence to learn to speak it well. It also takes prayer.
7. **Love Language** cannot be true if either person using it is drunk or high.
8. The **Love Language** of sexual intercourse is meant to express the total commitment of both partners to a lifelong relationship of love. Sexual intercourse, therefore, is true only within marriage.

My Personal Commandments

Think for a moment about your personal ideals and guidelines regarding sexuality and sexual activity. What will you have to do and what will you have to avoid in order to be sexually moral and responsible? The commandments that follow are meant to be a guide. Use this list to help you formulate your **personal commandments** about what you will and will not do as you grow toward sexual maturity.

I WILL NOT

1. **I will not** deliberately exploit any person for my own selfish sexual gratification.
2. **I will not** have sexual intercourse with any person except the one to whom I have committed myself in marriage.
3. **I will not** use the signs of affection—hugs, kisses, touches—in a non-loving way or simply as a means of arousing sexual feelings in myself or in another.
4. **I will not** put myself in any situation—time, place, activities, companions—in which I will be tempted to go beyond my personal sexual limits or those of my partner.
5. **I will not** use alcohol or any other drug that will impair my ability to think clearly and act responsibly in a dating situation.
6. **I will not** watch movies, use Web sites, look at magazines, read literature, or listen to music whose primary aim is to exploit or degrade sexuality.

7. **I will not** tease, encourage, pressure, or force another person to go beyond his or her personal moral limits.
8. **I will not** date a person with a reputation for casual sex or party with people who have such a reputation.
9. **I will not** deliberately fantasize or daydream about situations that are immoral and contrary to my personal value system.
10. **I will not** blame another person for my own failure to set limits for myself or for my lack of self-discipline in following those I have set.

I WILL

1. **I will** respect my sexuality as a precious gift from God to be used for my happiness according to the plan of God.
2. **I will** take time to think about my own personal, relational, and sexual ideals, and to establish for myself definite moral guidelines and limits.
3. **I will** follow the guidance of the Bible and the Church in creating and evaluating my sexual ideals, personal convictions, and moral guidelines.
4. **I will** develop a close personal relationship with God and pray every day for the grace and strength needed to live up to my personal moral convictions and ideals.
5. **I will** communicate openly with my parents or other trusted adults concerning my relationships and my efforts to live morally.
6. **I will** develop warm friendships with people of both sexes and learn to treat everyone with respect, sensitivity, kindness, and compassion.
7. **I will** continue to deepen my understanding of sexuality in all its facets—physical, emotional, social, psychological, and spiritual.
8. **I will** develop self-discipline in all aspects of my life and learn to postpone gratification, to practice self-denial, to sacrifice for others, to control my emotions and desires.
9. **I will** learn to act responsibly and reasonably, to be aware of the probable and possible consequences of my actions, and to make my decisions accordingly.

10. **I will** look to find much joy and happiness in the experience of falling in love. I will cherish with great tenderness the one I love and protect with all my strength the precious gift of love.

Just Say No

Sometimes teens think that "everybody" is having sex, especially the more popular "in" teens. The fact is that the majority of teenagers are not in relationships involving sexual intercourse. Young people who are well adjusted, highly motivated, and future oriented are far less likely to be sexually active than those with a low self-concept and low ideals.

A surprising number of young people are committed to remaining virgins until they marry. And many who have experienced sex are determined not to do so again before marriage. It takes a great deal of determination to hold on to such an ideal today. It also takes practice. It takes practice saying "no."

There are many situations in life in which we have to say "no" to our own wishes, as well as the desires of others. How would you "just say no" in the following situations? (In two of the items, the answer might be "Not until we are married" rather than "No." Which two?)

For Boys Only

1. You're at a party with a girl you've been dating for three months. She wants you to go upstairs to a bedroom with her. How do you **say no**?
2. Your girlfriend tells you that she has been saving herself for someone like you? How do you **say no** to her explicit message?
3. You want to have sex just once to find out what it is like. How do you **say no** to your own curiosity?
4. Your girlfriend, whose parents both work, wants you to come to her house after school. Knowing you will be tempted to have sex, how do you **say no** to this dangerous situation?
5. She tells you she loves you very much and wants to have your baby. How do you **say no**?
6. She says you don't have to worry about getting her pregnant because she is on the pill. How do you **say no** to sex anyway?

7. It seems like you're the only one of your friends who hasn't had sex. How do you respond to the subtle pressure in your own mind to be like everyone else and still **say no** to sex?
8. You're afraid that if you don't make sexual advances, she'll think you are gay? How do you **say no** to your own desire to have sex just to prove you are not gay?
9. You have gone too far with your girlfriend and are very much aroused. How do you **say no** to your own passions?
10. You are beginning to have feelings of sexual attraction for a close relative. How do you **say no** to your own feelings?
11. Your girlfriend is unhappy and you think sex will comfort her. How do you **say no** to your own desire to use sex to make her feel better?
12. Some of your friends want to have a contest to see who can "score" with the most freshman girls. How do you **say no** to this challenge?

For Girls Only

1. You like your boyfriend more than anyone else you've known, but now he tells you that "if you really loved me, you'd have sex with me." How do you **say no**?
2. You're sitting in the family room with your boyfriend, watching TV, and he begins to touch you erotically. How do you **say no** to his moving hands?
3. You're afraid if you don't have sex with him, he'll drop you and look for someone else. How do you **say no** to your own fear of losing him?
4. Your friend set you up with her boyfriend's best friend. He paid for dinner and the movies and now seems to feel that you should have sex with him. How do you **say no**?
5. He says you don't have to worry about getting pregnant because he'll use protection. How do you **say no** despite his reasoning?
6. He promises that if you get pregnant he will marry you. How do you **say no** anyway?
7. The college guy you met at a party wants to take you back to his dorm room. How do you **say no**?

8. Your relationship is beginning to fall apart and you feel that having sex will make it strong again. How do you **say no** to the temptation to use sex to keep him?
9. A relative you have always respected begins making sexual advances. How do you **say no** to him?
10. Your girlfriends tell you that you'll never be able to keep a boyfriend unless you have sex. How do you **say no** to their suggestion?
11. The man whose children you babysit is driving you home. He parks a block from your house and tries to kiss you. How do you **say no**?
12. You and your boyfriend are already sexually active, but you have been doing some serious thinking and you really want to stop. How do you **say no** the next time?

Personal Journal

- What ideas do you have for learning how to really love someone you are "in love" with?
- How difficult would it be for you to discuss your views about sex with a boyfriend/girlfriend? What might help you to open the discussion?
- Write three personal commandments that sum up your individual ideals and guidelines for sexuality and sexual activity.
- How often do you explain your personal moral convictions on sex? What are the occasions for this topic coming up?

9

A CRIMINAL CHOICE: SEXUAL ABUSE

The focus of this book has been to help teens make good decisions and choices regarding their sexuality. Unfortunately an alarming number of teens and children are not given a choice about engaging in sexual activity. Sex is forced upon them by someone older and stronger, often someone they know and love. In these situations sex is a degrading act of violence.

It is estimated that one in four girls and one in seven boys are sexually abused at least once by the time they are eighteen. In some cases, especially those involving incest, the abuse occurs on a regular basis for many years. The average age for sexual abuse is about ten or eleven, but children of all ages, even infants, have been molested.

The legal definition of sexual abuse includes any intentional touching of a person's intimate parts, either directly or through clothing, for the purpose of sexually arousing or gratifying, or sexually degrading or humiliating. The law also prohibits involving a minor in any sexually explicit conduct for the purpose of viewing, photographing, or video-taping.

The usual molester is not a strange man leaping out of the bushes or luring a child into a car. More than 80 percent of the time a sexual abuser is someone the victim knows. The usual child molester is an older male member of the child's immediate family—a father, stepfather, boyfriend of the mother, older brother, uncle, or cousin. He may even be a respected member of the Church and community.

For adolescent girls, the abuser is often a date or boyfriend. A recent survey reported that 65 percent of teen boys felt that it is okay to force sex on a girl if they have been dating for six months or longer.

This chapter deals with sexual abuse—personal accounts, its lifetime effects, ways to avoid abuse, and things to do if you or someone you know has been abused.

Note to Parents

This chapter addresses sexual abuse by sharing three stories of sexual abuse. It is estimated that one in four girls and one in seven boys are sexually abused by the time they are eighteen. Teens who are in or have been in such a situation should seek professional counseling. The chapter also suggests precautions teens can take to keep from being sexually abused in a variety of situations, including dating. Parents Anonymous (800-421-0353) is an agency that deals with child abuse. If your family faces this problem, seek help through this or a similar agency.

Three Stories

All of the following stories of sexual abuse are true, but the names in them have been changed.

Linda's Story[8]

> When Linda was ten years old, she would lie awake at night, dreading her father's visit to her bed. For two years he had been forcing her to do things that hurt her physically and confused her. She had tried going to bed with her clothes on, but this did not stop her father from bothering her.
>
> Linda never told anyone what her father was doing. She was afraid that if anyone knew, terrible things would happen to their family. Her father stopped abusing her when she put a lock on her bedroom door, but he then started going to her younger sister's bed.
>
> Now, seven years later, Linda is a seventeen-year-old mother. She admits that she has been a passive sexual partner with her boyfriends, agreeing to any kind of sex they request. She receives no pleasure from her sexual relationships, but she is willing to do what is expected to win her boyfriend's affection.
>
> Linda is a bright young woman with dreams for the future, but something keeps her from settling down.

She still feels guilty that she did not protect her sister and is afraid of what might happen to her own little girl.

Shane's Story[9]

(Shane relates this story as an adult looking back at a childhood experience.)

During the eleventh year of my life I was sexually molested by a close friend, a man I trust and admired. One August night Bill drove me from a meeting we both attended. My house was quiet and empty. My parents, sisters, and brother were visiting friends in another town and wouldn't return until very late. Bill pulled into our driveway, turned off the car, and asked for a tour of our house. I liked Bill and could tell he liked me; I was honored that he wanted to be with me. . . .

When I showed him my bedroom, he entered it and, pushing me playfully onto the bed, began tickling me. I stopped giggling when Bill started to remove my clothes and then removed his. I was frightened but also exhilarated. I didn't understand the mixed-up feelings swirling through me. Inside, I was screaming that this was wrong, but Bill was so gentle and soft-spoken that I didn't want to say no. He laughed at me and made me laugh. He kept teasing me about being so shy as I lay passively, quietly on the bed, shaking. I was too frightened to flee or fight and too confused to know if what Bill was doing was right or wrong. . . .

Karen's Story[10]

I really liked Jim a lot. One day he came over to my house and got a little too intimate. I told him that that was enough but he kept on. I told him no, and he said yes. I felt inferior to him because he was a big guy. He finally said yes, and carried me into the bedroom and forced me to have sex. Afterward he would never call or want to do anything with me. I felt used and abused.

It's one year later, and I'm now afraid of sex of any kind. I'm afraid to even kiss a guy. When I'm touched I jump and feel a shock inside of me. I have a boyfriend now, and I told him what happened to me. He wants to help me out but I'm afraid to let him. Maybe someday I'll go and seek counseling, or I'll have to face my fear on my own.

Effects of Sexual Abuse[11]

Sexual abuse almost always leaves deep emotional and psychological scars, not only on the victim but also on the offender. If you were abused as a child or a teen, understanding these effects can help you deal with your personal problems. If the sexual abuse was prolonged or very serious, you will most likely need professional counseling. Knowing about the difficulties associated with sexual abuse will also help you to understand a friend or family member who may confide in you that he or she has been abused.

Difficulties with trust

People who have been molested as children tend to have deep feelings of insecurity. They don't know whom they can trust and not trust. They tend to trust people whom they shouldn't and not trust people whom they could. They are even afraid to trust themselves, especially their feelings of love and affection.

Difficulties with self-protection

People who have been abused sexually often feel helpless and unprotected. They develop inappropriate ways to protect themselves from being hurt physically or emotionally. Some learn to turn off their feelings. Some act as though they don't need or want anything so they won't be disappointed or hurt again. Some become tough, aggressive, and hostile, or find other inappropriate ways to feel as if they have power and control.

Difficulties with self-esteem

Those who have been abused sexually often blame themselves for what happened. They feel worthless and unlovable; they feel dirty and used. Some people react by being driven to work harder so they can out-perform everyone else. Some just don't try, because they don't believe they can accomplish anything anyway. Some hold back from taking any kind of chances because it feels safer.

Difficulties with fitting in

People who have been abused sometimes protect themselves by staying isolated. They feel that as long as they don't have to relate to anyone else they will manage. They avoid letting people get to know them, automatically assuming that people won't like them. Some try to hide—by being too fat or too thin, by dying their hair purple or piercing a body part, by always staying home. Some react in the opposite way, attaching themselves to anyone who is halfway friendly or interested.

Difficulties with love relationships

Those who have been abused sexually have often had little experience in loving and being loved in a safe way. If the person who molested them is a family member, the victim can be emotionally confused, not knowing how to separate love and hate, anger and guilt. Because the signs of affection—caresses, touches, intercourse—have been used to hurt or belittle or control them, loving contact now triggers memories that are unpleasant and painful. If and when the person does learn to love someone, he or she tends to be over-demanding, needing constant reassurance and attention. Such people are often inordinately jealous and possessive.

Difficulties with sexual behavior

A disproportionate number of pregnant adolescents were victims of sexual abuse as children or teens.

Sexually abused girls have learned to be passive and accepting rather than risk offending the molester or causing disruption in the family. Experience has taught them that they have to "pay" for affection with sex. Sexually abused boys have learned to equate sex with power and control. These effects of sex abuse may well be a leading factor contributing to a large number of adolescent pregnancies.

Precautions Against Sexual Abuse—Points to Remember

Take precautions to limit the possibility that you might be sexually abused. Keep the following points in mind.

1. Your body is your sacred domain. You have a right to decide how it will be touched and by whom. No one is ever free to force, pressure, or tease you into having sexual contact of any kind.
2. Trust your own feelings. If someone's conduct or attitude seems suspicious, or if you are confused, afraid, and uncomfortable, there may be a good reason.
3. Have a clear idea of your own sexual values, goals, and ideals. Be assertive in saying no if you feel you are being pushed or pressured.
4. Don't weaken your defenses with alcohol or any other substance.
5. Don't walk alone at night. Don't hitchhike or accept rides from strangers.
6. Immediately leave a room if someone is there you can't trust.
7. Don't be alone with a date in a potentially dangerous place like an empty house or a parked car.
8. Refuse single dates with someone you don't know well and never go on a date with someone who has the reputation of being sexually abusive or immoral.
9. Never accept a drink you have not poured and never set your drink down or leave it unattended.
10. Avoid any situation you deem to be dangerous.

Post script:

- If you have been abused in the past and haven't ever talked about it, tell someone you trust, preferably a counselor or youth minister. You will probably need professional help to cope with the abuse, to put it in perspective, and to move on to a healthier way of relating to the world.
- If you or someone you know is ever involved in sexual assault, get help immediately. Both the victim and the offender will need professional help.
- If a friend tells you he or she has been abused in the past, be supportive and affirming, but do not try to counsel your friend alone. The problem is too big for you to handle. Encourage your friend to get professional help; if you can, take the person to a counselor yourself.

Personal Journal

- Write a list of all the situations you can think of that can be classified as sexual abuse.
- What would be your course of action if a close friend told you of being sexually abused?
- Name some other precautions a teenager can take to avoid being sexually abused.

10

A NON-CHOICE: SEXUAL ORIENTATION

Probably the most sensitive issue in the entire area of human sexuality is sexual orientation. Most people are attracted sexually toward persons of the opposite sex, but a few people—anywhere from two to five percent—experience sexual attraction toward persons of the same sex.

People who are predominately attracted to the opposite sex are said to be heterosexual. Those who are predominately attracted to the same sex are called homosexual.

Recent statements by the Catholic Church have addressed the difficulties faced by people with homosexual inclinations. The Catechism of the Catholic Church states:

> The number of men and women who have deep-seated homosexual tendencies is not negligible. They do not choose their homosexual condition; for most of them it is a trial. They must be accepted with respect, compassion, and sensitivity. Every sign of unjust discrimination in their regard should be avoided. These persons are called to fulfill God's will in their lives and, if they are Christians, to unite to the sacrifice of the Lord's Cross the difficulties they may encounter from their condition.
>
> (#2358)

This chapter contains a message to teens with homosexual inclinations. Even if you are sure you are heterosexual, hear the message thoughtfully. The information might help you to be more understanding and tolerant of others who have, or are thought to have, homosexual tendencies. You may someday be called on to advise a friend or loved one who has confided to you that he or she is homosexual.

Note to Parents

The aim of this chapter on sexual orientation is twofold: 1) to speak a positive Christian message to any young people in the group who feel that they have or might have homosexual inclinations, and 2) to help all of the young people, heterosexual and homosexual, to deal in a Christian way with the reality of homophobia—the irrational fear, hatred, and persecution of homosexuals. A special "Note to Parents of Homosexual Children" is included on pages 102–103..

Homosexuality

The following article reminds us of the need for sensitivity to teens who may be just discovering their homosexual orienation.

When we talk about homosexuality, it is very important to distinguish between homosexual tendencies and homosexual activity. Homosexuality is determined not by what a person does but what a person feels. A person who feels strongly and exclusively attracted to persons of the same sex is said to have homosexual inclinations, whether he or she ever acts on those feelings or not. A person who performs genital sexual actions with someone of the same sex is engaging in homosexual activity, whether the person has a homosexual or heterosexual orientation. Persons who engage in sexual activity with both sexes are called bisexuals.

A person does not have a choice about his or her sexual orientation. Sexual attraction just happens—it is part of our physical and emotional makeup. Some time in their early teen years, most young people begin to discover that they are sexually attracted to the other gender. The awakening of sexuality is a confusing and unsettling period for all teens. For those teens who begin to have sexual feelings toward members of the same sex, this period is all the more troubling.

Try for a moment to put yourself in the position of the adolescent who suspects or knows that he or she has homosexual inclinations. Try to imagine what it must be like to discover during your adolescent years that you might be a homosexual, one of those people that so many of your peers, and even adults, make jokes about, put down, pick on, condemn.

Though we don't have a choice about our sexual tendencies, we do have a very clear choice about our sexual activity. Unlike sexual orientation, sexual activity can be moral or immoral, depending on circumstances. The Catholic Church teaches that all sexual activity outside of a valid heterosexual marriage is morally unacceptable and therefore wrong or sinful. This would include premarital sex, masturbation, and homosexual genital behavior.

Since marriage between homosexuals is not an option, homosexual persons are called to a life of celibacy. As Christians, we are all called to be especially sensitive to the trials and difficulties faced by homosexuals and to the effect negative words and actions must have on them. These issues are multiplied during the teen years. If you were a homosexual teenager, what should you be hearing today from your teachers, from your heterosexual friends, from your parents, from your Church?

Homophobia

Review the definition and characteristics of homophobia as you analyze your own attitudes towards homosexuals.

Homophobia is defined as "the irrational fear and hatred of homosexuals." Homophobia is found in individuals, groups, or whole societies. It takes many forms:

- violent dislike or hatred of homosexual persons
- fear of associating with homosexuals
- an irrational fear of being considered "gay"
- vulgar and abusive language and jokes about homosexuals
- physical violence against homosexual people
- condemnation, discrimination, and persecution of homosexuals

The Church is strongly opposed to the kind of negative behaviors that are characterized as homophobia. In Always Our Children, the Bishops of the United States wrote:

> Respect for the God-given dignity of all persons means the recognition of human rights and responsibilities. The teaching of the Church makes it clear that the fundamental rights of homosexual persons must be defended and that all must strive to eliminate any form of injustice, oppression, or violence against them.

A Message to Teens with Homosexual Inclinations

The following message is written directly for any homosexual teens who may be reading this book. If you are a heterosexual, please read the message thoughtfully as a way of learning to be sensitive to this invisible minority.

Sometime over the past few years you've made a frightening discovery about yourself. You're different. Your feelings and interests and daydreams aren't like everybody else's. While all your friends are going crazy over the opposite sex, you find yourself being sexually attracted to people of your own sex.

You don't want to admit it even to yourself, but you think you might be homosexual. You're afraid. You're confused. You feel absolutely isolated. You don't want anyone to know. You don't have anyone to talk to. You don't know where to turn for help.

Here are some things you need to know about yourself and the rest of society.

- **First and foremost, you need to know that you are good. You are loved by God just the way you are.** We don't know why some people are homosexual and some heterosexual, but we do know that God loves and accepts each of us in all of our uniqueness. We are all special to God. Whatever combination of factors caused some of us to be heterosexual and some homosexual, God is eager to help each of us to grow from where we are to where God wants us to be—strong and loving individuals. What matters to God is what each of us does with the unique set of characteristics we are blessed with.

- **You also need to know that you are not alone.** Even using the lowest estimates of social scientists for how many people have a homosexual orientation, there are thousands of gay and lesbian people in North America alone. There are homosexual doctors, homosexual lawyers, homosexual musicians, homosexual athletes, and homosexuals in all the more mundane jobs of society. There are very likely several homosexual teachers and students in your school. These people may choose to keep their sexual orientation hidden, but you probably know and admire several of them.

- **You need to know, and probably already know, that growing up homosexual can be very difficult.** Homophobia—the irrational fear and hatred of homosexuals—is a pervasive part of the world you live in; you will never be able to completely escape its effects. But that very difficulty can enhance your chances of maturing as a beautiful human being. Because you know yourself to be different from most of your peers, it can be easier for you to resist peer pressure, to stand on your own two feet, to make your own decisions.

  On the one hand, don't over-emphasize your homosexuality. It's only one part of the total package that is you. On the other, your life experiences can help you to develop a loving sensitivity to people's feelings, your own and those of others. The special difficulties you face can lead you to deepen your spiritual life, and to be serious about life and its questions. Many homosexual teens are leaders in their class or youth group. They tend to be self-directed and self-motivated and often excel in their studies, in athletics, and in the arts.

- **Don't decide too soon that you are homosexual.** The awakening of sexuality can be a turbulent, confusing time for many young people. Sometimes heterosexual teens experience strong sexual feelings or crushes toward attractive people of the same sex, especially admired adults or older teens. Heterosexual teens sometimes get involved in sexual experimentation with people of both sexes. An isolated homosexual experience or relationship is not a clear indication of homosexual orientation.

- **There are people you can talk to about your sexual questions and worries.** Many teachers and counselors in your school, many pastors, and many youth ministers would be open and accepting if you came to them with questions about your sexual orientation.

- **There are also support groups for homosexual youth and their parents** that have the approval of the Church. You can get in touch with such a group by calling your diocesan office. Talking to the people in these organizations will provide you with understanding and support as you learn to deal with your homosexuality in the months and years to come. The people in these groups will also be able to help you face what is often one of the biggest problems for homosexual teens—telling your parents about your sexual orientation.

- Even though you didn't have a choice about your sexual orientation, **you have many choices to make about the responsible use and development of your sexuality**, just as your heterosexual peers do. You need to understand clearly the difference between the four kinds of relationships represented by the letters L.I.F.E.—Love, Infatuation, Friendship, and Exploitation (see pages 19–23). And you need to learn to make positive moral choices based on that distinction.

- The basic relationship during your high school years should be friendship. Every teen, homosexual or heterosexual, should develop many friendships with people of both sexes, people of different ages, and people from a variety of racial, religious, economic, and cultural backgrounds. **A homosexual teenager who is outgoing and friendly can often be one of the most popular teens in school—with many male and female friends.**

- For both heterosexuals and homosexuals, one of the primary tasks of adolescence is to learn how to deal with the relationships represented by the "I"—infatuation and sexual intimacy. **Catholic moral teaching is the same for homosexual teens as heterosexual teens—genital sexual activity outside of marriage is forbidden.** Social expectations cause difficulties in this area for both homosexuals and heterosexuals, but in different ways. Society is too accepting of sexual activity among teenager heterosexuals, and absolutely condemnatory of any kind of sexual relationship for teenage homosexuals. As a Christian, you will need to learn how to live a sexual life that is life-giving and love-giving—and in accord with God's plan for you. For both homosexuals and heterosexuals this requires self-discipline, responsibility, personal sacrifice, and God's grace.

- The temptation all humans face is **exploitation**. We are all capable of exploiting or using another person for our own sexual gratification. Promiscuous sex, casual sex, experimental sex, sex just for the excitement—all of these are forms of sexual exploitation. Both homosexual and heterosexual teens need to be aware that involvement in **any kind of non-loving, non-committed sexual activity is morally, physically, and psychologically dangerous** for you and for your sexual partner.

- And, of course, the most fulfilling and enriching human relationship is love. All of us need to realize that we are lovable, that we are loved, that we are capable of loving others. **The constant challenge for every individual is to learn to be a truly loving person—unselfish, thoughtful, forgiving, compassionate, generous**. A homosexual person is every bit as capable of developing and sustaining deep love relationships as heterosexual persons. No matter what other differences we might have, the one reality that unites us all as human beings and children of God is love.

- As a homosexual teen, you need to know most of all that **the future is wide open to you**. Homosexuality imposes some limitations on you, but these are certainly not insurmountable. Your life can be richly satisfying for yourself and a great gift to your brother and sister human beings. Be the good and beautiful person you were created by God to be.

Church-Sponsored Counseling Services for Homosexual Teens

Name	Phone
Name	Phone
Name	Phone

For Parents of Homosexual Children

The following recommendations are by the United States bishops to parents of homosexual children.[12]

1. Accept and love yourselves in order to accept and love your son or daughter. Do not blame yourselves for a homosexual orientation in your child.
2. Do everything possible to continue demonstrating love for your child. However, accepting his or her homosexual orientation does not have to include approving of all related attitudes and behavioral choices. In fact, you may need to challenge certain aspects of a lifestyle that you find objectionable.
3. Urge your son or daughter to stay joined to the Catholic faith community. If they have left the Church, urge them to return and be reconciled to the community, especially in the sacrament of penance.
4. Recommend that your son or daughter find a spiritual director/mentor who will offer guidance in prayer and in leading a chaste and virtuous life.
5. Seek help for yourself, perhaps in the form of counseling or spiritual direction, as you strive for understanding, acceptance, and inner peace. Also, consider joining a parents' support

group or participating in a retreat designed for Catholic parents of homosexual children. Other people have traveled the same road as you, but may have journeyed even further. They can share effective ways of handling delicate family situations such as how to tell family members and friends about your child, how to explain homosexuality to younger children, how to relate to your son or daughter's friends in a Christian way.

6. Reach out in love and service to other parents who may be struggling with a son or daughter's homosexuality. Contact your parish about organizing a parents' support group. Your diocesan Family Ministry Office, Catholic Charities, or special diocesan ministry to gay and lesbian persons may be able to offer assistance.
7. As you take advantage of opportunities for education and support, remember that you can only change yourself; you can only be responsible for your own beliefs and actions, not those of your adult children.
8. Put your faith completely in God who is more powerful and more forgiving than we are or ever could be.

Personal Journal

- How do you understand the Church's position on homosexuality?
- To what degree are you homophobic? A lot? A little? Not at all? How does it show?
- If you found out your college roommate was homosexual, what would you do?
- What do you think would be the hardest part about being a homosexual teenager?

11

FORGIVENESS: A HEALING CHOICE

Sex isn't over when it's over. Whether it is a positive or negative experience, engaging in sexual intercourse usually has deep and long-lasting effects on the two people involved, especially the female.

Sex is a gift from God, a share in God's own creative power. God built into our bodies the powerful sexual urges that attract us to one another. God also gave us the ability to control and direct our sexual drives. The divine plan is that we should use our sexual energy to foster love and produce life.

But sex often becomes a source of sin rather than love. Sex can be selfish and irresponsible, vulgar and destructive. It can be used to exploit, to humiliate, to conquer. The use of sex in a way that is contrary to God's plan is always sinful.

The Bible very clearly condemns adultery, fornication, and other sexual sins. Fornication, the biblical term for premarital sex, is mentioned fifty-six different times in the New Testament. Every time it is used it is strongly condemned.

Exploitative and irresponsible sex frequently has long-range negative consequences for both the person who sins and the one who is sinned against. This chapter introduces some of the entanglements that irresponsible, sinful sex can cause in the lives of teenagers and follows up with how forgiveness of self and others is a way to bring about the healing of those hurts.

Note to Parents

In many secular sex education programs for teens, only the physical long-term consequences of sexual activity outside of marriage are discussed. This chapter discusses other negative consequences of sexual behavior, including emotional and spiritual consequences. This chapter is also meant to encourage any teens who have been sexually active to begin to practice chastity again and to understand that God is always close at hand to offer his forgiveness and healing.

Sexual Sin

The following letters from teens show some of the entanglements that irresponsible sex can cause in the life of teens.

> I really believed he loved me when we did it, but two months later he dropped me for his old girlfriend. I felt as if I had 200 knives go through me.
>
> TINA—16

> The day my girlfriend had the abortion was the most traumatic day of my life. I couldn't talk to her at all after that. I just felt absolutely alone. I couldn't even talk to God.
>
> JAMES—17

> When I was twelve, I was forced to have sex with someone much older than me. Later on I started to act out sexually. Sex had the biggest role in my life. It's why I have HIV today, I think.
>
> COURTNEY—19

> So many feelings—betrayal, regret, hurt, anger. Sometimes now I feel so distant from him, I wonder why we were together in the first place. But here I am, pregnant with his baby.
>
> SYLVIA—17

> I had no choice. I was forced into an abortion by my parents. Till this day it still bothers me, especially whenever I see a baby, but I was told never to talk about it.
>
> GRETCHEN—18

> I don't know if it's always a bad thing to have sex, but I do know it's bad to turn to sex when you are trying to substitute it for something else in your life that is missing. I have been guilty of doing that.
>
> FERNANDO—16

We were in this cabin at camp, and I started making out with Tricia. I was so drunk I didn't know what I was doing. I woke up in the morning, and she was still lying next to me. I felt like trash. It ruined our friendship.

LEWIS—15

Afterward I felt so guilty. I didn't have any intention of staying with her. I just used her for sex.

BRAD—16

I didn't object to what he was doing because I was too tired and too drunk. I didn't even know the guy. What if he had AIDS or something. I never felt so guilty and dirty in my entire life. I just wanted to climb out of my own body.

YVONNE—18

I was sixteen when I first had sex. I think everyone thinks it's going to be wonderful the first time. In all the movies it seems that way. I know my first time wasn't like that.

MARNIE—17

The guy was cute but I didn't really like him. I was just stringing him along to see how far things would go. Afterward I think he felt embarrassed and ashamed. But I knew it was my own fault.

ANGELA—17

She was telling me to stop, but I didn't think she meant it. I just kept going at her. I couldn't believe how much force I had. I pinned her down and did it. She was crying and sobbing, but I didn't even care. I only realized fully what I had done after she was gone. I don't know how she can ever forgive me. God either.

TODD—18

> I thought he was going to leave me, like other guys have done. But he didn't. Maybe he does love me. Or maybe he loves the baby. Or maybe his parents told him to stay with me.
>
> ERICA—18

Sometimes the results of sexual sin are tangible. Sylvia is left with an unplanned pregnancy. Gretchen's baby has been aborted. Erica has a baby and a boyfriend she is not sure loves her. Courtney had a deadly disease (and has since died). Yvonne may be infected with HIV. Lewis's friendship with Tricia is ruined.

Often, however, the negative consequences are more subtle and pervasive. Marnie was disappointed her sexual experience did not live up to how she imagined sex would be. James feels isolated from everyone, even God. Tina suffers from betrayal and rejection. Todd, Angela, Brad, and Fernando are burdened with guilt.

God's response to the negative consequences of sin is to offer us a way to overcome them. The Bible teaches us that God is especially compassionate and forgiving toward those who sin sexually. Remember the woman Jesus met at the well, who was living with her sixth husband? (See John 4:4–42.) Remember the woman who was caught in adultery and dragged before Jesus? (See John 8:1–11.) In both cases Jesus responds to the women with understanding and comfort rather than condemnation.

Jesus doesn't deny that the women have sinned. He explicitly tells them not to sin again. But he seems to be aware that the sin in their lives is not simply an individual choice. Both women were caught in a tangle of sinfulness that was beyond their full control. Other people are involved in their sins, and the women are not only sinners, but victims as well. Jesus realizes that they need both forgiveness and healing.

Forgive Us . . . As We Forgive

The following reflection is meant to remind you of the power of forgiveness that God offers to each of us to heal the hurts we may have caused others and that others may have caused us. Refer to this meditation when you are in need of forgiveness and healing.

The scriptures show clearly that God deals with the effects of sin in our lives by offering us forgiveness and healing. Forgiveness is at the heart of Christianity. Jesus taught us to pray: "forgive as we forgive," and he instructed us to forgive our offenders seventy times seven times. He showed us how to forgive when he forgave those who had crucified him.

In order to be healed of the effects of sin in our lives, we need to be forgiven for the hurts we have inflicted on others. To help understand what seeking forgiveness involves, think of some people you have hurt at one time or another—people you may have used, abused, betrayed, disappointed, manipulated, taken advantage of, lied to, lied about, cheated, injured, or violated in any way.

Concentrate on one of the people who may still be feeling the pain of your actions. Imagine you and this person in the presence of God. Tell God how you feel about the situation now. Try to imagine how that person must feel about you. Picture yourself standing in front of this person, holding out your hand in friendship and apology. Pray for the grace of forgiveness and ask Jesus to forgive you, to help the other person forgive you, and to help you to forgive yourself.

Forgiving those who have offended us involves a similar process. Again, think of a few people who have hurt you—people who have used you, abused you, put you down, taken advantage of you, lied to you, disappointed you, betrayed your trust, or made fun of you.

Concentrate on one person who has hurt you deeply. Try to imagine that you and this person are in God's presence and that God is looking lovingly at both of you. Tell God how you feel about your troubled relationship with this person.

Try to imagine how the other person feels about having hurt you. Think positively and try to realize that this person really wants to do what is right but, like you, sometimes fails. Think of Jesus hanging on the cross out of love for you both. Hear him say, "Father, forgive them, for they know not what they do." Try to become aware of the mercy God extends to the other, and to you, and pray for the grace needed to forgive the one who has hurt you. Ask Jesus to open your heart so you can love the one who has hurt you, and pray for a new sense of peace between you.

> The process of forgiving and being forgiven is a source of emotional and spiritual healing. But it is also possible that problems may surface that are serious enough to require long-range professional and spiritual counseling in order to be healed. A school counselor or parish minister can guide you in finding that kind of help.

Personal Journal

- How has your own experience, or the experience of people you know, taught you that premarital sex is sinful and hurtful?
- What are some long-term consequences of sex that have affected your peers?
- Which do you find most difficult: forgiving others, accepting the forgiveness of others, or forgiving yourself? Explain.

12

LOVE CHOICES

"Making love" is an expression often used to describe having sex. Unfortunately making love and loving someone are often not the same thing.

Real love desires what is best for the other person. As St. Thomas Aquinas described, "To love is to will the good of another."

Real love is committed. When you really love someone you are with the person for the long haul. As the bride and groom promise to one another: "I will be true to you in good times and in bad . . . to love you and honor you all the days of my life."

This chapter describes many types of love, most of which you will experience for yourself as you move through life. The chapter also reminds you that God has expressed his love for you by offering you the very best gift of all, the gift of himself.

Note to Parents

This final chapter reminds the teens that "making love" is not the same thing as loving. Real love is committed love. The activities of the chapter point to the God of love as the model for all types of real love, including many examples of love that do not include sex. The teens are taught in several different ways that in spite of any failings, God loves them very, very much.

God Is Love

An excellent place where we can turn to learn about the mystery of love is the Bible. One of the most famous passages tells us that God is love.

> Beloved, let us love one another, because love is of God; everyone who loves is begotten by God and knows God. Whoever is without love does not know God, for God is love. In this way the love of God was revealed to us: God sent his only Son into the world

so that we might have life through him. In this is love: not that we have loved God, but that he loved us and sent his Son as expiation for our sins. Beloved, if God so loved us, we also must love one another. No one has ever seen God. Yet, if we love one another, God remains in us, and his love is brought to perfection in us.

—1 JOHN 4:7–12

Experience Is the Best Teacher

When it comes to learning about love, experience is definitely the best teacher. Each time you love someone, each time you are loved, you get new insights into the wonderful mysterious experience called love. You can also learn much about love by seeing how it affects the lives of other people.

The following "love stories" are about people and events the author has known or known about. The stories depict different kinds of love choices, but the various kinds of love overlap: marital love is a form of Gospel love, betrothal love is a form of romantic love and an incomplete form of marital love, all loves have an aspect that is forgiving love, etc. As you read the stories, think about the love choices that have touched your own life and of the ways you, too, have learned from experience what real love is all about.

Parental Love

The alarm yanked Mrs. Garcia awake and she pulled herself out of bed and onto the cold floor. The nights were so short since she started that second job. She pounded on the door of the girls' room on the way to the bathroom. Tuition was the problem—or at least one of the problems. She really wanted the girls to go to St. Mary's. They loved it there, and besides, she had gone to a Catholic high school and it seemed even more necessary in today's world. But since the divorce, money was really tight.

She picked up a pile of dirty underwear and stuck it in the hamper. It would be easier if the girls would have a better attitude, she thought. She needed them to babysit the little kids and help with the housework. But she'd rather do those things herself than listen to their constant whining and arguments.

She wanted so much to have a loving family. But most of the time she felt she was the only one who cared.

Family Love

Gene is a big guy. Not athletic and robust. Not fat and sloppy. Just big. He's one of those people no one pays much attention to at school. He has a few friends. He gets so-so grades. He's been out with a girl once or twice.

But there is one person who thinks Gene is wonderful—his little sister Elizabeth. Gene remembers well the day four years ago when he found out his mother was pregnant. At last, after twelve years of being an only child! He waited for the baby to be born with secret excitement.

And his life has never been the same since. Their parents both work, so Gene and his little sister spend lots of time together. He likes taking care of her, playing with her, hearing her laugh, seeing her little personality blossom. He loves the way she comes running to him when she gets hurt.

Gene can't imagine any brother loving a little sister more than he loves Elizabeth.

Romantic Love

Luke has never known anyone quite like Megan. He had looked at other girls at school, even talked to a few of them, but his friends knew that Luke just wasn't the romantic type before Megan.

Luke remembers every detail about that first afternoon. He was hanging out in the gym after freshman basketball watching the cheerleaders practice their routines. He noticed Megan because she kept messing up. It was the good-natured way she laughed at her mistakes that caught his attention. Then, just to be crazy, he took her hand and helped her up into the formation.

That was it. He touched her hand, she smiled at him, and his knees turned to rubber. Luke waited around to walk her home, and they laughed all the way to her house.

Luke can't believe how easy it is to talk to her. And she's so much fun to be with. He and Megan have gone everywhere and done everything together for two whole weeks.

And tonight, Luke has definitely decided, he's going to get up the courage to kiss her.

Married Love

Twenty-five years. It was hard to believe they had really been married for a quarter of a century. Cecilia looked over at her husband sprawled out on the couch. "Where has the time gone?" she asked herself. Two children married. One in college. The youngest in high school. And Brian, the family dropout, loafing around the house instead of looking for a job.

"For better or worse," they had promised on that sunny June day so long ago. Little did she know then what those words would mean. She and Peter had definitely had their share of "worse": Becky, their oldest daughter, pregnant at seventeen; Jim arrested for drug possession his senior year; Brian refusing to go to school; Peter himself losing his job at the mill after twenty-one years.

Each new problem put a strain on their relationship. But they had learned to love when the loving was hard—to love beyond the blaming and the disappointment and the pain.

And the "better?" That too was much better than she would have ever imagined. Peter was such a gentle husband and father. In the early years, she thought, it was sharing their role as parents that brought them closest to each other—watching the children grow together, worrying about them together, being proud of them together.

But now it was the steady comfort of knowing Peter could be counted on as a friend, to be there for her, to feel things with her, to support and encourage and challenge her. "I'm a lucky woman to be married to such a man," she told herself, then she smiled wryly. It had taken a lot of forgiving to come to that point—on his side and on hers.

Cecilia took the casserole out of the oven and called her husband to the table. He kissed her playfully on the nose before he sat down to eat. "Are you remembering what day it is, my love?" She laughed. "I sure am," she said, "and I'm getting ready to start working on the next twenty-five years."

Betrothed Love

Exactly three weeks from today she would be Mrs. Dominic Mercado. Patti crossed off one more date on the calendar, and mentally went through the long list of things she still had to do before the wedding.

It was hard to imagine herself married to Dom, but even harder to think of being separated from him. She had been going with him for so long—five years if you counted the summer they were just friends. They had made it through the separate college problem, writing faithfully twice a week and calling every weekend.

Patti was very much in love with Dom. He was so respectful, so thoughtful, so much fun. And so spiritual. They had decided together that they wouldn't have sex until they got married, but Dom had been the strong one whenever things started getting heavy. Not many girls today could say that about their boyfriends, she thought. Patti remembered clearly the way he had explained it on their engaged couple's retreat. "At first chastity was a moral decision," he had told their discussion group. "Now it is a love decision. It is my love of God and of Patti.

Patti and Dom worked together to plan every detail of their wedding—the Mass, the dinner, the dance. But Patti alone had made the plans for the wedding night, even to picking out the music they would make love to. She felt a strange mixture of confidence, apprehension, and joy as she thought about it all. Only three short weeks and she would give herself completely to the man she loved.

Vowed Celibate Love

It isn't something she can explain. Not to herself. Certainly not to her mother. But Chris is sure that this is what she wants to do with her life. She has known for a long time that God has to play a central role in whatever she does. She loves her family. She loves her friends. She even thought for a while that she would marry Tad. But the idea of being a nun has just kept tugging at her heart.

The turning point in her decision came two summers back. She had always been proud of her Native American heritage, but six weeks on a Sioux reservation left her with a whole new awareness of the beauty of her people—and their poverty. She loved the children in her religion classes, but she could see how little hope the future offered them.

Chris has no doubt that God is calling her to spend her life helping her people. Next week she will take her vows in the community of sisters who work on the reservation.

Tough Love

"Not again," Curt groaned. He could tell by the way Theresa rattled the keys against the door that she was drunk. It was the fourth day this week she had stopped for a cocktail after work. Curt knew the pattern well. Now she would come in, head straight for the liquor cabinet, plunk down in front of the television, and drink until she passed out.

Her last binge had lasted two months and almost cost Theresa her job. Curt was afraid her supervisor was getting wise to his excuses, and he was tired of calling in and lying for her. "At least," he thought, "she never hits the kids when she's drunk. She just ignores them."

Theresa was such a wonderful mom to Stacy and little Aaron when she was sober. And Curt loved her so much. But it was going to take something desperate to get her to go for help. Curt had threatened many times to take the kids and leave her, but the threats didn't work anymore.

He didn't even look at Theresa as she stumbled into the kitchen. He just walked past her and went upstairs to pack some things for himself and the children.

Friendship Love

Jason hopped off his bike and bounded up the front steps of Rogerio's house. The place was bustling as usual, little kids on the faded couch watching TV, Rogerio's mom in the kitchen peeling potatoes, the dog wildly yapping his welcome. Things were so different here than at his own home, Jason thought as he waited for Rogerio to finish his shower. But he loved it here. He and Rogerio has been friends since fourth grade. They did everything together: school, homework, football, youth group, even girls. Rogerio was much more than the brother he'd always wanted. Jason was the first person Rogerio had called when his dad was killed in a factory accident last year. And Jason knew he could trust Rogerio with his life if it ever came to that. He was absolutely certain that they would be friends forever.

Forgiving Love

Al brushed the tears back and walked slowly up the front steps of the funeral parlor. He dreaded the next few minutes. Certainly this would be more difficult than any criminal charges he faced. How could he face Mrs. McBride?

His best friend Skip McBride was dead and it was his fault. Al had been over the accident in his mind a thousand times. The country road. The dark corner. The stop sign he didn't see until too late.

If only he and Skip had left the party early. If only he hadn't insisted he was sober enough to drive. If only it had been him and not Skip. If only his best friend was still alive! His throat tightened. What could he say to Skip's mom? Her husband last year, and now her only son.

Al pushed open the heavy door and moved into the crowded room. She was standing up in the front near the casket, quietly greeting people in line. He watched her for a long time, trying to find in his mind some words he could say to her. He was amazed at her strength. She was so calm, so dignified.

He was near the front of the line when she noticed him. For a moment she stood death still, and the color drained from her face. "Mrs. McBride," Al blurted out the words in choking sobs. "I'm so sorry."

Skip's mother just stepped forward and tenderly folded him into her arms.

Gospel Love

It was the first really cold day in fall. Ted slipped into a front seat on the city bus, directly across from the old woman. He had seen her before, usually on his way home from school. But this time Ted really noticed her for the first time.

The woman's tired face was lined with deep wrinkles. Her hair was long and scraggly, and her dress was a dirty gray. She was wearing a bulky old sweater with leather patches that only partly covered the rips on the elbows. But Ted was especially aware of the old woman's shoes. They might have been men's dress shoes and were so badly worn that her callused bare feet stuck through them in several places.

Ted couldn't help noticing the contrast between those old shoes and the elite—and expensive—athletic shoes he had bought last week. He put the woman out of his mind and tried to nap. But every time the bus lurched, he'd open his eyes and catch her feet and his own in his line of vision.

What happened next, Ted can't explain very well. As they approached his home corner he reached down and loosened his laces. When the bus stopped, Ted slipped off his new shoes, handed them to the astonished woman, and hopped off the bus in his stocking feet.

God's Love

A man had two sons and the younger son said to his father, "Father, give me a share of your estate that should come to me." So the father divided the property between them. After a few days, the younger son collected all his belongings and set off to a distant country where he squandered his inheritance on a life of dissipation.

When he had freely spent everything, a severe famine struck that country, and he found himself in dire need. So he hired himself out to one of the local citizens who sent him to his farm to tend the swine. And he longed to eat his fill of the pods on which the swine fed, but nobody gave him any. Coming to his senses he thought, "How many of my father's hired workers have more than enough food to eat, but here am I, dying from hunger. I shall get up and go to my father and I shall say to him, "Father, I have sinned against heaven and against you. I no longer deserve to be called your son; treat me as you would treat one of your hired workers." So he got up and went back to his father.

While he was still a long way off, his father caught sight of him, and was filled with compassion. He ran to his son, embraced him and kissed him. His son said to him, "Father, I have sinned against heaven and against you; I no longer deserve to be called your son."

But his father ordered his servants, "Quickly bring the finest robe and put it on him; put a ring on his finger and sandals on his feet. Take the fattened calf and slaughter it. Then let us celebrate with a feast, because this son of mine was dead, and has come to life again; he was lost and has been found."

—Luke 15:11–24

How Do I Love Thee?

God loves you. How can you show your love for God?

The Call
Jesus says, "Come, follow me."
I say,
"Lord, you're calling the wrong person.
I'm not the following type.
It takes me all my time
to stand on my own two feet."
And he says, "I love you."
I say,
"Now, don't get me wrong, Lord.
I do all I can within reason,
but I can't afford to go overboard.
I mean, I have to live in this world."
And he says, "I love you."
I say,
"It's all very well to talk about love,
but love is dangerous.
It can get people crucified.
At the best it can be misunderstood.
If I go round telling people I love them,
someone's going to lock me up."
And he says, "I love you."
I say,
"The trouble is, I'm not ready.
Come back in a few years
when I've got my life sorted out.
By then I should have something
to offer you."

And he says, "I love you."
I say,
"Lord, don't look at me like that.
You're making it very difficult.
All right, I'll spell it out.
I'm a sinner. I'd let you down.
I'd give my life to you
and then try to take it back again.
I'm weak, Lord."
And he says, "I love you."
I say,
"You don't understand what I'm telling you.
I'd deny you and betray you.
There'd be times when I'd crucify you.
And what would you think of me then?"
And he says,
"I love you."

(JOY COWLEY, EVERYTHING 'ROUND US IS PRAISE, AVE MARIA PRESS, 1997)

Personal Journal

- Write about a love choice that has touched your life in one of the kinds of love shared in this chapter.
- Name some things you can do to be more loving toward the important people in your life.
- Write a prayer, telling God what you will do to love him more.

EPILOGUE

CREATED FOR LOVE— A CONCLUDING MEDITATION

Find a quiet spot—a back pew in an empty church, a secluded bench by the lake, a cozy corner in your own room.

Try to be as still as you possibly can—quiet your body, quiet your voice, quiet your mind. Listen to the rhythm of your breathing. Feel the regular pulsing of your heartbeat.

When you are very still, begin to read the following reflection. Read it slowly, thoughtfully. Pause often to think about what you are reading. Let the message sink deeply into your mind and heart.

> Imagine that you are holding a tiny seed in your hand—so small that you can barely see it. Once you were a microscopic seed. Try to imagine back the fourteen, sixteen, or eighteen years to when your life first began. Picture a young woman, your mother, and a young man, your father, deeply in love with one another. And picture the Creator making you out of their love.
>
> Imagine the tiny being that was you planted in your mother's womb, drawing life and nourishment from her body. See the loving Creator there, tending the seed, guiding its growth. Watch the embryo develop—a tiny head is formed, little arms and legs with perfect little hands and feet, a tiny beating heart, eyes that will someday see, ears that can hear even in the womb.
>
> Within three or four months, by the time your mother knows you are there, you look almost like a very tiny baby just three inches long, curled up inside the womb. Cup your hand and imagine that you were once small enough to fit within your palm.

Think now about the day that you were born. Imagine God standing before your parents, offering you to them and saying, "I give this child to you today as a gift of my love."

See your mother holding you for the first time, your father cradling you in his arms. Think about how joyful and excited your family must have been to hear the news of your birth. Picture each of your grandparents, your aunts and uncles, your older brothers and sisters, all smiling and cooing over you.

God created you out of love. God created you for love. Call to mind the many ways your family loved you in those early years, and the ways you learned to show your love for them. Can you see yourself at two, climbing into Daddy's lap for a good-night hug? Or yourself at four, running to Mommy with a skinned knee? Try to feel your parents' loving arms around you still.

Remember first grade—making a Valentine that said, "I love you, Mommy" to hang on the refrigerator door. Remember third grade—picking out the perfect birthday present for your dad.

Imagine God your Creator watching you over the years as you grew into a loving, caring person. See God smiling at your attempts to be thoughtful and kind, and patiently forgiving all the times you were selfish, thoughtless, and mean.

But perhaps there were times along the way when you weren't loved the way you should have been. Maybe you were hurt, disappointed, neglected, or even abused by the people who were supposed to love you. Try to realize how much God cared for you even then, and how lovingly God now offers you tender healing.

Now focus on the present. Imagine that the God who created you for love is standing before you at this very moment, holding out to you a small treasure chest. God says your name, "_______, I offer you this precious gift. It is part of my very self, a portion of my greatest power. I share with you the power to create and nourish human life."

Imagine yourself reaching out to accept the treasure chest from God. Hear him say: "Treasure this precious gift—your sexuality. Let the energy that radiates from it help you to become a truly loving person. And then, someday, share this treasure with one special person as a gift of your love."

Be very still, thinking about God's words to you. Over the past few years you have been discovering within yourself the powerful reality of your sexuality. Be aware of this gift within you now, and try to realize as deeply as you can that it is, indeed, a gift from God—a gift that comes from love and is meant for love.

Then spend a few moments talking to God within your heart. Tell God how much you want to become a truly loving person. Thank God for the gift of life, the gift of love, the gift of sex.

If you have ever misused God's gift, pray for forgiveness, asking God to heal whatever hurt has been caused to you or to someone else. If someone else has spoiled your gift in any way, ask God to heal your memory of the pain and guilt and shame of that time. And pray for forgiveness for the person who harmed your precious treasure.

And finally, pray that God will bring into your life the beauty and the joy of real love. Ask God to help you to become a truly loving person and to send you someone wonderful to love. Promise God that no matter what has happened in the past, from this moment on you will use the treasure of your sexuality always and only as a gift of love.

Helpline Numbers

If you have questions or problems concerning your sexuality or other aspects of growing up, it may be helpful to talk with a caring, competent adult. Listed below are the names and numbers of people who are willing and able to help you with common problems.

Pregnancy Counseling

______________________________ Phone ____________________

Pregnancy Testing

______________________________ Phone ____________________

NOTES

1. Ministry to Persons with a Homosexual Inclination: Guidelines for Pastoral Care, United States Conference of Catholic Bishops.
2. Love Waits (Fall Christian Action Council: Falls Church, VA).
3. These statistics are taken from the Alan Guttmacher study, 1995, and the March of Dimes study, 1998.
4. This exercise is adapted from Teen Pregnancy by Donna and Roger Ewy (Boulder Colorado: Pruett Publishing, 1984).
5. See www.usccb.org/comm/archives/2007/07068.shtml.
6. Evangelium Vitae 62.
7. Both quotations are taken from Sex, Love, and You by Tom and Judy Lickona (Notre Dame: Ave Maria Press, 1994).
8. Linda's Story is adapted from "Child Sexual Abuse: A Hidden Factor in Adolescent Sexual Behavior," the report of a study done for the Illinois Department of Children and Family Services, 1986.
9. Shane's Story is taken from an anonymous column printed in Isthmus (Madison, WI: 1986).
10. Taken from an anonymous note written to the author by a teen on retreat at her center.
11. Information drawn from Outgrowing the Pain by Eliana Gil (San Francisco: Launch Press, 1983) and Sexual Molestation: A Handbook for Professionals by C. Barnes and J. Shaffer.
12. "Always Our Children: A Pastoral Message to Parents of Homosexual Children and Suggestions for Pastoral Ministers" (A Statement of the Bishops Committee on Marriage and Family, National Conference of Catholic Bishops, 1997).

Sr. Kieran Sawyer, S.S.N.D., is widely known and respected for her work with teens. She is Director Emeritus of TYME OUT, a retreat center near Milwaukee, Wisconsin, and a regular presenter at workshops and conferences in the areas of adolescent sexuality and catechesis. Sr. Kieran's materials are well-known in engaging the feelings, minds, and faith of teens—lessons, activities, and prayers that "really work" with teenagers.